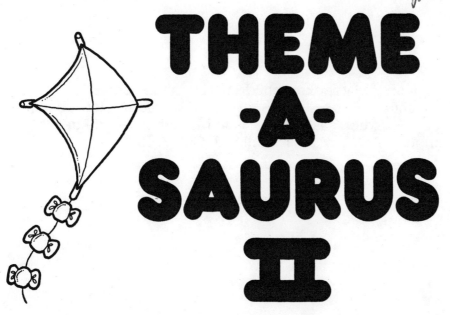

THEME -A- SAURUS II

The Great Big Book of More Mini Teaching Themes

Compiled by **Jean Warren**

Illustrated by **Gary Mohrmann**

Warren Publishing House, Inc.
Everett, Washington

Special thanks to Jeannie Lybecker, children's literature specialist, for compiling a list of children's books for each unit. For information about these books or other children's literature, write Ms. Lybecker at Early Childhood Bookhouse, P.O. Box 2791, Portland, OR 97208.

Editor: Gayle Bittinger
Contributing Editor: Elizabeth McKinnon
Editorial Assistant: Susan M. Sexton
Layout and Cover Design: Kathy Jones

ISBN 0-911019-26-X

Library of Congress Catalog Number 89-51179
Printed in the United States of America
Published by: Warren Publishing House, Inc.
           P.O. Box 2250
           Everett, WA 98203

INTRODUCTION

Share the Gift

The world is filled with wondrous toys,
Treasures all, for girls and boys.
Ants and dirt and wheels and snow
Are nourishment for minds to grow.
So share the treasures, share the glee,
Share the gift – curiosity.

Jean Warren

After the tremendous success of *Theme-A-Saurus,* I am pleased to present *Theme-A-Saurus II.* It is filled with new teaching units that offer more opportunities for hands-on learning experiences for young children, more treasures to explore and more opportunities to capture those magic teaching moments when children are ready to learn.

Each unit contains a collection of activities from a variety of curriculum areas such as art, science, language, learning games, movement, music and snacks. All of the ideas are developmentally appropriate for young children and use only inexpensive, readily available materials.

Providing even more opportunities for learning and growing, *Theme-A-Saurus II* makes it easy for you to share the gift of curiosity.

Jean Warren

CONTENTS

CONTENTS

CONTENTS

Giant Ant Hill

Cut a giant ant hill shape out of brown butcher paper and place it on the floor. Help the children draw rooms and tunnels all over the ant hill. Let them add ant prints as described below.

Ant Prints – Set out several black ink pads and give each child a new unsharpened pencil. To make an ant print, have each child press the eraser end of his or her pencil on the ink pad, then make three prints in a row on the ant hill shape. Let the children make as many ant prints as they like. Help them use black felt-tip markers to add six legs to each ant.

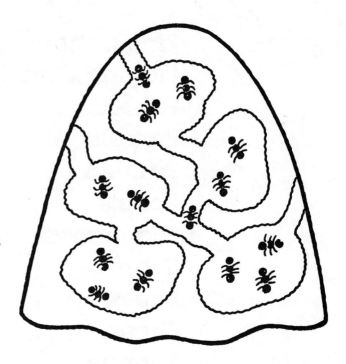

Ants in Nests

Number the bottoms of six paper baking cups from 1 to 6 and place them in a 6-cup muffin tin. Give the children 21 raisins or small black buttons to use for ants. Let them place the appropriate number of ants in each paper baking cup "nest."

The Ants Go Marching

Sung to: "When Johnny Comes Marching Home"

The ants go marching one by one,
Hurrah! Hurrah!
The ants go marching one by one,
Hurrah! Hurrah!
The ants go marching one by one,
Watching ants is lots of fun,
So let's all go marching
One by one by one.

Additional verses: "The ants go marching two by two/ Worker ants have lots to do; The ants go marching three by three/ The ants all live in a colony; The ants go marching four by four/ Now they're marching through the door; The ants go marching five by five/ Now it's time to say 'Goodbye!' "

Adapted Traditional

Ant Search

Take the children on a search for ants to observe them in their natural habitat. Ants tend to make nests under boards, rocks or leaves. Be sure not to disturb the nests. (Children are less likely to destroy a nest after watching how diligently the ants work to build it.) If you can't go to the ants, try making them come to you by placing a juicy piece of fruit outside as bait. Return to the fruit an hour or so later with the children to watch the ants that have found it. Place a tiny piece of the fruit a short distance away and you may have a chance to see two ants working together to carry it to their nest.

Ant Farm

Invite the children to accompany you on a search for ants. When you find some, let the children help you carefully scoop the ants and some dirt or sand into a plastic bag and twist the top closed. Take the ants back to your room and allow them to calm down for a few minutes. Then transfer them to a large clear plastic box (the kind that shoes are stored in). Heat the sharp end of a nail and press it against the box lid to make a hole. Make several holes. Fill the holes with cotton and tape the lid securely to the box. Let the children observe the industrious ants, but be sure to cover the box with a cloth when the ants are not being observed. (This keeps the ants from digging deep tunnels to escape the light.) Once a week let the children place a small amount of jelly, fruit or honey mixed with water through one of the holes, removing the cotton first and replacing it after feeding. Every three days have them add about a teaspoon of water through one of the holes with an eyedropper. When the children's study of ants is over, let them help you carefully return the tiny creatures to their natural habitat.

Variation: For individual ant farms, purchase small clear plastic containers with lids. Punch holes in the tops of the containers and write a child's name on each one. Let each child collect and feed the ants as described above.

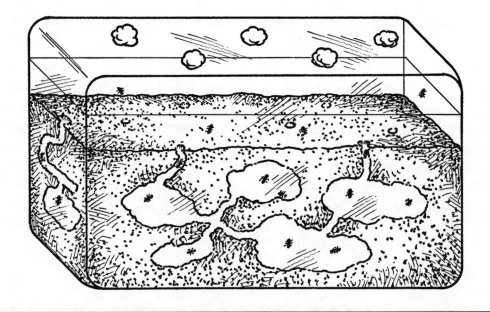

Ants-On-A-Log

Let the children help make "logs" by filling celery sticks with peanut butter. Then give them each three or four raisin "ants" to place on top of their logs.

Variation: For a different kind of stuffing, have the children mix together equal portions of peanut butter, grated carrots and crushed shredded wheat. Let them press the mixture into celery sticks and then place raisins on top.

Children's Books:
- *Ant Cities,* Arthur Dorros, (Harper Row, 1987).
- *Anteater Named Arthur,* Bernard Waber, (Houghton Mifflin, 1967).
- *Two Bad Ants,* Chris Van Allsburg, (Houghton Mifflin, 1988).

Contributors:
Sue Foster, Mukilteo, WA
Ellen Javernick, Loveland, CO
Susan M. Paprocki, Northbrook, IL

BLOCKS

Printing With Blocks

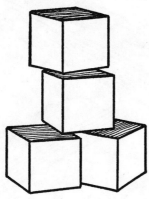

Use sandpaper to smooth the rough edges of several different sizes and shapes of blocks of wood. Make paint pads by folding paper towels, placing them in shallow containers and pouring on small amounts of tempera paint. Give the children the blocks and pieces of construction paper. Let them dip the blocks into the paint and then press them on their papers to make prints.

Block Sculpture

Have the children sit in a circle and place a box of blocks to one side. Have one child begin by choosing a block from the box and placing it in the middle of the circle. Then let the children take turns choosing blocks and adding them to the first one to create a block sculpture. When all the blocks have been used, put them back in the box and start all over again.

Alphabet Blocks

Print simple words on index cards. Place the cards and a set of alphabet blocks on a table. Let the children select word cards and find blocks with letters that match the letters in the words.

Variation: Have the children write their names on large index cards (or write their names for them). Then let them match the alphabet blocks to the letters in their names.

Following Directions

Arrange chairs in a circle and put a box of blocks in the center. Invite each child to select a block from the box and find a chair to sit on. Then give the children directions to follow, such as "Put your block on top of your head; Put your block under your chair; Put your block beside your chair."

BLOCKS

Counting Blocks

Number five index cards from 1 to 5. Give each child five blocks. Hold up one of the cards and ask the children to identify the number on it. Then have them each count out that many blocks.

Block Shapes

Use a felt-tip marker to trace around several different sizes and shapes of blocks on a piece of posterboard. Let the children take turns matching the blocks to the corresponding tracings.

Block Area Game

Make a game out of cleaning up the block area. Cut construction paper in the shape of each kind of block and tape the shapes on the shelves where the blocks are stored. When the children put the blocks away, have them place each block on the shelf that contains the matching construction paper shape.

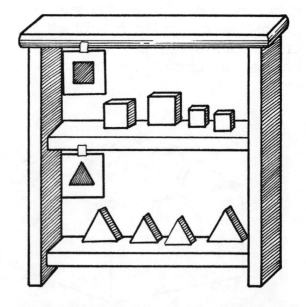

Picking Up Blocks Today

Sung to: "Ten Little Indians"

Pick up the blocks and put them on the shelf,
Pick up the blocks and put them on the shelf,
Pick up the blocks and put them on the shelf.
Picking up blocks today.

Jean Woods
Tulsa, OK

Find a Block

Sung to: "If You're Happy and You Know It"

Find a block that's square over there,
Find a block that's square over there.
Find a block that's square and hold it in the air,
Now put away your block over there.

Find a block that's round, without a sound,
Find a block that's round, without a sound.
Find a block that's round and touch it to the ground,
Now put away your block, without a sound.

Gayle Bittinger

Children's Books:
- *Block City,* Robert Louis Stevenson, (Dutton, 1988).
- *Line Up Book,* Marisabina Russo, (Greenwillow, 1986).
- *Changes, Changes,* Pat Hutchins, (Macmillan, 1971).

Contributors:
Betty Ruth Baker, Waco, TX
Joleen Meier, Marietta, GA

Rolling Designs

Give the children pieces of yarn or string to dip into bowls of glue. Have them wrap the glue-covered yarn around short cardboard tubes any way they wish. Allow the glue to dry. Make paint pads by placing folded paper towels in shallow containers and pouring on small amounts of tempera paint. Let the children roll their tubes across the paint pads, then all over pieces of construction paper.

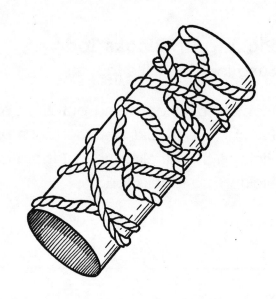

Tube Chains

Let the children use felt-tip markers to decorate short cardboard tubes. When they have finished, flatten the tubes and cut slits in them as shown. Have the children stretch out their tubes by pulling on the ends. Then show them how to fold down the areas between the rings to create chains.

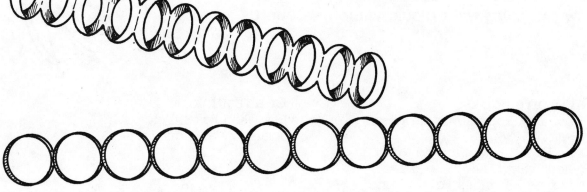

Color Scopes

Cut small squares out of several different colors of cellophane. Put each square over the end of a short cardboard tube and fasten it in place with a rubber band. Let the children look through the tubes. Ask them to describe how the world looks through the different colored scopes.

Tube Puppets

Cut cardboard tubes into 4-inch sections. Turn the tubes into simple characters by drawing on facial features with felt-tip markers and adding yarn hair. Glue a Popsicle stick handle to each tube. Let the children use the puppets while singing songs or telling stories.

CARDBOARD TUBES

Clip the Tubes

Cut cardboard tubes into 2-inch lengths. Set out the tubes and a box of clothespins. Have the children use the clothespins to clip the tubes together anyway they wish. Or encourage them to try making simple shapes such as worms or flowers.

Variation: Ask the children to clip specific numbers of tubes together.

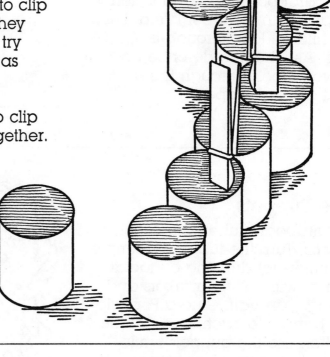

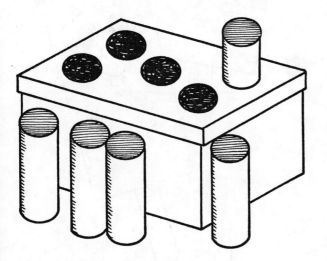

In and Out

Cut five 2-inch circles out of the lid of a shoebox. Put the lid on the box and tape it in place. Set out the box and five cardboard toilet tissue tubes. Let the children take turns putting the tubes in the holes and taking them out again.

Cardboard Tube Props

Let the children use cardboard tubes for dramatic play. The tubes can become telephones, telescopes or megaphones. Tape two short tubes together to make a pair of binoculars. Or add crepe paper streamers to the end of a long tube to create a magic wand.

Snack Tubes

Cut cardboard tubes into 4- to 5-inch sections. Put small amounts of trail mix, cereal, pretzels or dried fruit in plastic sandwich bags and insert them in the tubes. Then wrap each tube in a piece of tissue paper and tie the ends with yarn or ribbon. Give the tubes to the children at snacktime.

Children's Books:
- *Little Red Riding Hood*, Brothers Grimm, (Holiday, 1983).
- *The Three Bears and 15 Other Stories*, Anne Rockwell, (Crowell, 1979).

Contributors:
Ellen Javernick, Loveland, CO

Feathered Friends

Cut chick shapes out of yellow construction paper. Give the children paint brushes and glue and have them use the brushes to spread glue all over the chick shapes. Then let them cover the glue with yellow feathers (available at craft stores). Have them complete their chicks by adding construction paper eyes and beaks.

Baby Chicks

Give each child one egg cup cut from an egg carton and two cotton balls. Put a mixture of baby powder and yellow powder tempera paint in a paper bag. Let the children take turns shaking their cotton balls in the bag, then carefully removing them and tapping off the excess powder over a sink or a trash basket. Have the children glue their yellow cotton balls in their egg cups, one on top of the other. Then let them add construction paper beak shapes and eyes to complete their baby chicks.

Variation: You may wish to use yellow cotton balls for this activity. Colored cotton balls are available at some drugstores and variety stores.

Chick Sequence Cards

Make sequence cards showing the different stages of a chick hatching. Draw pictures of the egg in its nest, the egg cracking, the chick partly out of the egg and the chick completely hatched. Mix up the cards and give them to the children. Let them put the cards in order.

Hatching Chicks

Discuss with the children how chicks hatch. Talk about the mother hen who lays the eggs, then sits on them to keep them warm. Tell the children about the baby chicks who begin tapping at their shells with their beaks until the shells crack and the chicks are able to wiggle out. If you can, take the children to visit a farm that has baby chicks. Let the children watch the chicks toddling around, eating food and drinking water.

Little Chick

As you recite the poem below, have the children act out the movements described.

Snuggled down inside
An egg that was white,
Was a tiny little chick
With its head tucked in tight.

Then it lifted its head,
Tapped the egg with its beak,
And quickly popped out –
Peep, peep, peep!

Colraine Pettipaw Hunley
Doylestown, PA

Chicken, Chicken

Have the children sit in a semi-circle and place a chair in front, facing away from the children. Choose one child to be the Chicken and have him or her sit in the chair. Place a plastic egg under the chair. Quietly choose one child to "steal" the egg from the Chicken and sit back down in the semicircle, holding the egg behind his or her back. Then have all the children put their hands behind their backs and pretend to have the egg. While the children chant "Chicken, Chicken, who's got your egg?" have the Chicken turn around and begin guessing who might have it. When he or she guesses correctly, let the child with the egg be the new Chicken.

Whose Nest?

Cut five mother hen shapes, five nest shapes and fifteen egg shapes out of felt. Number the hens from 1 to 5. Glue a different number of eggs (from 1 to 5) on each nest shape. Place the nests and the mother hens on a flannelboard. Let the children help the mother hens find their nests by counting the eggs and matching each hen to the appropriate nest.

Down at the Barnyard

Sung to: "Down by the Station"

Down at the barnyard,
Early in the morning.
See the little chicks,
Moving to and fro.
See them flap their wings
As they come to greet us.
Flap, flap, flap, flap,
Off they go.

Jean Warren

Children's Books:
- *Good Morning Chick,* Mirra Ginsburg, (Greenwillow, 1980).
- *Rosie's Walk,* Pat Hutchins, (Macmillan, 1971).
- *Chicken Little,* Steven Kellogg, (Morrow, 1985).

Deviled-Egg Chicks

Remove the shell from a hard-boiled egg and cut the egg in half lengthwise. Scoop out the yolk into a small bowl. Mix the egg yolk with mayonnaise and mustard to taste. Fill each egg white with half of the yolk mixture. Add two raisins and a small piece of carrot to each yolk mixture to make eyes and a beak. Makes 2 servings.

Contributors:
Sue Foster, Mukilteo, WA
Colraine Pettipaw Hunley, Doylestown, PA

Clothespin Sponge Painting

Cut sponges into 2-inch pieces. Pour small amounts of different colored tempera paint into small containers. Give each child a spring-type clothespin, a sponge piece and a piece of paper. Have the children clip their sponges to their clothespins. Then let them hold their sponges by the clothespins, dip the sponges into the paint and dab them on their papers to create designs.

Clothespin Recipe Holders

Have each child glue a spring-type clothespin on a smooth flat rock. When the glue has dried, let the children paint their rocks and clothespins, if desired. Then have them each glue two small plastic moving eyes on their clothespins near the clip ends.

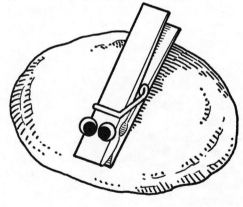

Clothesline Fun

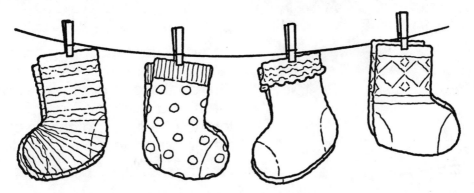

String a piece of yarn between two chairs to make a clothesline. Collect several pairs of socks, each with a different color or pattern. Put the socks and some clothespins in a basket and place it near the clothesline. Let the children take turns finding matching pairs of socks in the basket and hanging them up with the clothespins.

Variation: Use sock shapes cut from a variety of colors of construction paper instead of real socks.

Clothespin Counting Game

Number five paper plates from 1 to 5. Attach a matching number of circle stickers around the rim of each plate. Set out the plates and fifteen spring-type clothespins. Let the children take turns selecting a plate, identifying the number on it and clipping one clothespin over each sticker.

Hint: For a more durable game, cover the plates with clear self-stick paper.

CLOTHESPINS

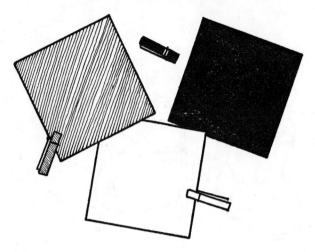

Color Clips

Cut 6-inch squares out of three or more different colors of posterboard. Paint four spring-type clothespins to match each square. Mix up the clothespins and place them in a box or a basket. Then let the children match the colors by clipping the clothespins to the sides of the appropriate squares.

Clothespin Relay

Divide the children into groups of three or four. Give each group a spring-type clothespin and a box of several small items (at least two for each child). Have the children stand in their groups on one side of the room. Place an empty box for each group on the other side of the room. When you say "Go," have the first child in each group use his or her clothespin to pick up one of the items in the group's box, walk quickly across the room and drop the item in the empty box. Then have the child walk quickly back across the room and give the clothespin to the next child in line. Have the children continue until all the items have been transferred to the boxes across the room. Then let each group count the number of items in its box.

Snap, Snap, Snap

Sung to: "This Old Man"

Snap, snap, snap. One, two, three,
We can all snap, look and see.
With a great big snap and little snaps too,
Watch us snap this song for you.

Give the children spring-type clothespins
and let them snap away as you sing the
song.

Jean Warren

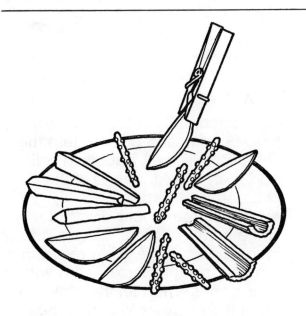

Snappy Snacks

Give each child a clean spring-type clothespin and a plate. Set out a variety of snack foods that the children can pick up with their clothespins and put on their plates. Suggested snacks are carrot and celery sticks, thin apple slices and pretzels.

Children's Books:
- *The Day Jimmy's Boa Ate the Wash,* Trinka Noble, (Dial, 1980).
- *The Nightgown of the Sullen Moon,* Nancy Willard, (Harcourt, 1983).

Contributors:
Barb Johnson, Decorah, IA
Brooke Keleman, Bellingham, WA

Cloud Dough

Mix together 6 cups flour and 1 cup salad oil. Add enough water to make the dough soft and pliable. If desired, add food coloring. This dough is soft and elastic and does not harden. Keep it in covered containers or plastic bags. Let the children play with the cloud dough. Encourage them to think of different ways to describe how it feels.

Hint: Have the children wear smocks to protect their clothes from the oil in this dough.

Cloud Art

Give each child a piece of light blue construction paper. Help the children fold their papers in half and then unfold them. Let the children use eyedroppers to squeeze three or four drops of white tempera paint on one side of their papers. Have them refold their papers and rub across them with their hands. Then let the children open their papers to reveal their cloud pictures.

Cloud in a Jar

Find a clear glass half-gallon or gallon bottle and a cork or rubber stopper that fits in its mouth. Poke a hole vertically through the stopper. Rinse the bottle with warm water and immediately insert the stopper. Blow as much air as possible into the bottle through the hole in the stopper. Cover the hole with a finger. Pull the stopper out quickly and let the children watch as a cloud forms inside the bottle. The cloud forms because there was a change from high air pressure (when the bottle was filled with air) to low air pressure (when the stopper was removed).

Cloud Pairs

Draw pairs of different shaped clouds on index cards. Mix up the cards and let the children take turns finding the matching cloud pairs.

Counting Clouds

Fluff out fifteen cotton balls. Glue from one to five of them on five pieces of light blue construction paper. Let each child have a turn counting the clouds on each piece of paper.

CLOUDS

Did You Ever See a Cloud?

Sung to: "Did You Ever See a Lassie?"

Did you ever see a cloud
A cloud, a cloud?
Did you ever see a cloud
That looked like a bear?
A big one, a little one,
A lazy one, a funny one?
Did you ever see a cloud
That looked like a bear?

Did you ever see a cloud,
A cloud, a cloud?
Did you ever see a cloud
That looked like a plane?
A big one, a little one,
A fast one, a slow one?
Did you ever see a cloud
That looked like a plane?

Help the children make up additional verses.

Jean Warren

When I Look Into the Sky

Sung to: "Twinkle, Twinkle, Little Star"

When I look into the sky,
I can see the clouds go by.
They don't ever make a sound,
Letting wind push them around.
Some go fast and some go slow,
I wonder where the clouds all go.

Frank Dally
Akeny, IA

Clouds in the Breeze

Clear a large space in the center of the room and have the children stand a few feet apart from one another. Then play music and let the children pretend that they are clouds drifting across the sky and changing shapes. Gradually increase the tempo of the music until the clouds are twirling and spinning around as if driven by the wind. Then gradually decrease the music's tempo until the drifting clouds finally come to rest in the sky.

Whipped Cream Clouds

Let the children watch as you use a rotary beater or an electric mixer to whip cream. Add sugar to taste, if desired. Serve the whipped cream "clouds" on top of sliced berries.

Children's Books:
- *Dreams*, Peter Spier, (Doubleday, 1986).
- *Cloud Book*, Tomie DePaola, (Holiday, 1975).

Contributors:
John M. Bittinger, Everett, WA

COTTON BALLS

Cotton Bunnies

Cut bunny shapes out of various colors of construction paper and give one to each child. Then give the children cotton balls and show them how to gently pull them apart. Have the children glue the fluffy cotton all over their bunny shapes. Let them glue on construction paper eye and nose shapes and pipe cleaner whiskers, if desired.

Cotton Ball Trees

For each child roll a piece of green construction paper into a cone shape. Secure with tape and trim the bottom of the cone so that it will stand with the pointed end up. Give each child a paper cone and several cotton balls. Have the children fluff out their cotton balls and glue them to their cones to make snow-covered trees.

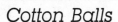

Cotton Ball Snowflakes

Tape a large sheet of blue construction paper or blue butcher paper on a wall at the children's eye level. Let the children glue white cotton ball "snowflakes" on the blue paper to make a winter-time scene.

Cotton Ball Snow Pal

Cut two large circles out of white butcher paper, making one slightly smaller than the other. Place the circles on a low table. Let the children work together to glue cotton balls all over the circles. When the glue has dried, attach the circles to a bulletin board, with the smaller circle above the larger one, to make a snow pal. Decorate the snow pal with facial features and clothing shapes cut from construction paper.

Cotton Ball Walk

Place cotton balls in a small plastic swimming pool. Let the children take turns walking through the cotton balls in their bare feet. As they do so, ask them to describe how the cotton balls feel.

Cotton Ball Counting Games

Give each child ten cotton balls. Have the children line up their cotton balls in different numbered rows.

Number five large index cards from 1 to 5 by drawing one circle on the first card, two circles on the second card and so on. Put the cards and fifteen cotton balls on a table. Let the children take turns placing one cotton ball on top of each circle on the cards. Then have them count how many cotton balls are on each card.

Place cotton balls in a sack. Let the children each take a turn reaching into the sack and grabbing a handful. Together, count how many cotton balls each child has taken.

Let the children fill small containers such as jewelry boxes, yogurt cups or sandwich bags with cotton balls. Then have the children empty their containers and count the number of cotton balls that were inside.

Cotton Ball Toss

Place one or two large containers on the floor and have the children stand 3 to 4 feet away from them. Let the children take turns tossing cotton balls into the containers.

Blowing Cotton Balls

Give each child a cotton ball. Have the children get down on their hands and knees and blow their cotton balls across the floor.

Children's Books:
- *Here Comes Peter Cottontail,* Jack Rollins, (Farrar, Straus and Giroux).
- *Runaway Bunny,* Margaret Wise Brown, (Harper, 1972).
- *Morning, Rabbit, Morning,* Mary Caldwell, (Harper, 1982).

Contributors:
Jane M. Spannbauer, South St. Paul, MN
Saundra Winnett, Lewisville, TX

Coupon Collages

Let the children tear or cut out a variety of coupons. Have them look for coupons of different sizes, shapes and colors. Give the children pieces of construction paper and glue. Let them arrange and glue their coupons on their papers.

Coupon Savers

Give each child a long white envelope. Let the children decorate their envelopes with crayons or felt-tip markers. Provide each child with a variety of coupons to put in his or her coupon-saver envelope. Let the children give the coupon savers to their parents as gifts.

Coupon Cubes

Cut twelve index cards to fit in the sides of two clear plastic photo cubes. Glue six different coupons to six of the index cards and put them in one of the photo cubes. Put six cards with matching coupons glued to them in another photo cube in a different order. Then let the children move the cubes around to find the matching coupons.

Coupon Sorting

Find several coupons for each of three or four different products. Put the coupons in a pile and let the children sort them according to product.

Variation: Have the children sort coupons by size.

Coupon Books

Give each child a book of several coupons stapled together. Let the children "read" their books by looking at the pictures and naming the products or by identifying the numbers on the coupon pages.

Coupons and Products

Collect empty product containers and coupons that match them. Tape the containers closed and cover the coupons with clear self-stick paper, if desired. Set out the product containers and the coupons. Let the children take turns selecting a coupon and finding the corresponding product container.

Extension: Set up a Grocery Store with the product containers and let the children use the coupons to "buy" them.

Cents-Off Snacks

Have the children work together to choose coupons for foods they like. Use the coupons to purchase the items at the grocery store. (If desired, let the children go to the store with you.) Then have the children help prepare the foods they selected for a meal or for snacktime.

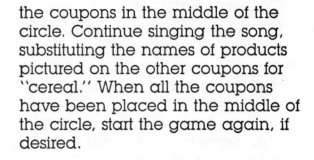

COUPONS

Coupon Song Game

Have the children sit in a circle and give them each three or four coupons. Include several cereal coupons among those you hand out. Sing the first verse of the coupon song. Then have the children with the cereal coupons hold them up and sing the second verse of the song before placing the coupons in the middle of the circle. Continue singing the song, substituting the names of products pictured on the other coupons for "cereal." When all the coupons have been placed in the middle of the circle, start the game again, if desired.

Sung to: "The Muffin Man"

Do you have a cereal coupon,
A cereal coupon, a cereal coupon?
Do you have a cereal coupon?
Show me if you do.

Yes, I have a cereal coupon,
A cereal coupon, a cereal coupon.
Yes, I have a cereal coupon,
Here it is for you.

Jean Warren

Variation: Let the children take turns asking one another for coupons by singing the song. They could ask for their favorite food coupons or for coupons that match those they are holding.

Coupon Money

Find a coupon for each of the following cents-off values: 25 cents, 50 cents, 75 cents and one dollar. Glue each coupon to a large index card. Place a quarter on the 25-cent coupon card and trace around it. Then trace around two quarters on the 50-cent coupon card, three quarters on the 75-cent coupon card and four quarters on the one-dollar coupon card. Set out the cards and ten quarters. Have the children place the corresponding numbers of quarters on the cards. Help them to understand that 25 cents means one quarter, 50 cents means two quarters and so on.

Coupon Hunt

Have the children sit in a circle and put an assortment of coupons in the middle. Call out a child's name and the name of a product pictured on one of the coupons.

Have the child hunt for that coupon. If necessary, help the child find the coupon by giving directions. Continue the game until every child has had a turn.

Children's Books:
- *Muskrat, Muskrat Eat Your Peas,* Wilson, (Simon and Schuster, 1989).
- *Tight Times,* Barbara S. Hazen, (Viking, 1979).
- *No Peas for Nellie,* Chris Demarest, (Macmillan, 1988).

Contributors:
Valerie Bielsker, Lenexa, TX

Grazing Cows

Cut cow shapes out of construction paper. Give each child one of the cow shapes and a piece of blue construction paper. Collect several bottles of glue. Then take the children outside and have them sit in a grassy area. Talk about how cows like to eat the grass that grows in their fields. Have the children glue their cow shapes to their papers. Then let them pick blades of grass and glue them on their papers for their cows to "graze" on.

Dairy Products Game

Ask the children to name as many foods as they can that are made from cows's milk, such as ice cream, Cheddar cheese, yogurt, whipped cream and Mozzarella cheese. Tell them that foods made from milk are called dairy products. Then play this game with them. Name a food that you like to eat. If that food is a dairy product have all the children "Mooo" as loudly as they can. If the food is not a dairy product have them shake their heads.

Variation: Instead of naming foods, show pictures of dairy products and other foods.

Milking Cows

Let the children experience what it would be like to milk a cow by hand. Put up a clothesline outside about 3 feet off the ground. Fill several disposable plastic gloves with water and poke a tiny hole in each fingertip. Hang the gloves from the clothesline and place a bucket and a stool under each glove. Have the children sit on the stools. Then show them how to squeeze the fingertips of the gloves to make the water squirt into the buckets.

Extension: Take the children to a farm and let them watch a cow being milked.

Cow Count

Cut several cow shapes out of felt. Arrange a piece of yarn in a circle on a flannelboard to represent a fence. Then place the cow shapes on the flannelboard as you tell the children a story that involves counting. For example, you might begin your story like this: "Two cows were standing in a field inside a fence. Another cow came and stood beside them. How many cows are inside the fence now?

Two cows left to find better grass to eat. Now how many cows are inside the fence?"

This Is the Way ✓
Sung to: "The Mulberry Bush"

This is the way we milk a cow,
Milk a cow, milk a cow.
This is the way we milk a cow,
Early in the morning.

Sandra Andert
San Diego, CA

Milk the Cow ✓
Sung to: "Row, Row, Row Your Boat"

Milk, milk, milk the cow
While sitting on a stool.
Pulling, squirting, pulling, squirting,
Till the bucket's full.

Pat Beck
Red Lion, PA

Who Says "Moo, Moo?" ✓

Sung to: "The Muffin Man"

Oh, do you know who says moo, moo,
Says moo, moo, says moo, moo?
Oh, do you know who says moo, moo?
The milk cow says moo, moo.

Oh, do you know who gives us milk,
Gives us milk, gives us milk?
Oh, do you know who gives us milk?
The milk cow gives us milk.

Susan Nydick
Philadelphia, PA

Orange Delight

Blend ¼ cup unsweetened frozen orange juice concentrate, ½ cup plain yogurt and ½ cup milk together in a blender. Pour into small cups to serve.

Celery Stuffing

Mix cottage cheese with grated carrot and chopped green onions. Cut celery into 4- to 5-inch long sticks and fill each one with a spoonful of the cottage cheese stuffing.

Children's Books:
- *Daisy*, Brian Wildsmith, (Pantheon, 1984).
- *Milk Maker*, Gail Gibbons, (Macmillan, 1985).
- *Blossom Comes Home*, James Herriot, (St. Martin, 1988).

Contributors:
Sandra Andert, San Diego, CA
Susan Peters, Upland, CA
Suzanne Thompson, Whittier, CA

Shiny Crabs

Give each child a piece of finger-paint paper or white shelf liner. Dribble some corn syrup on the children's papers and sprinkle on small amounts of yellow and red powder tempera paints. Let the children fingerpaint with the gooey mixture. Then allow the papers to dry overnight. In the morning they will have a shiny colored surface similar to the surface of a crab's shell. Cut the papers into crab shapes and hang them on a wall or a bulletin board.

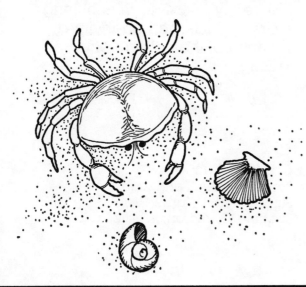

Crab Facts

Crabs live on rocky, muddy or sandy seashores. Each crab has ten legs, four on each side of its body and two big claws, or pincers, in front. Crabs use their legs to walk sideways across the rocks and sand. They also molt every year, which means that they shed their old shells and grow new ones.

Crawling Crab

Cut a crab shape, as shown above, out of posterboard. Use a hole punch to punch a hole in the center of one side. Tie one end of a 4-foot piece of yarn to the leg of a chair sitting on carpet. String the crab on the yarn. Position the crab shape so that the hole is away from the chair leg. Let the children take turns holding the free end of the yarn about 6 inches off the floor and raising and lowering it slightly to make the crab crawl.

Directions Game

Draw a small picture of a crab on a piece of paper (or cut one out of a magazine) and cover it with clear self-stick paper. Set out four rocks of different shapes, sizes and colors. Give one child the crab picture and ask him or her to put the crab "on top of the biggest rock," "underneath the round rock" or "beside the black rock." Then give the crab to the other children, one at a time, asking each child to put the crab in a different place.

Variation: Put the crab in a specific place and ask the children to tell you where the crab is.

Five Little Crabs

Recite the following poem with the children:

One little crab, lonely and blue,
It met another crab, now there are two.

Two little crabs living near the sea,
Out crawled another, now there are three.

Three little crabs went off to explore,
They soon found another, now there are four.

Four little crabs, glad to be alive,
They found a new friend, now there are five.

Five little crabs went for a walk,
And all at once they spied a rock.

Now five little crabs are as happy as can be,
Under a rock by the deep blue sea.

Marie Wheeler
Tacoma, WA

Eating Like Crabs

Explain to the children that crabs grab food with their pincers when they want to eat. Give the children crackers and ask them to eat like crabs, using their thumbs and index fingers as pincers.

Crab Walk

Ask the children to sit on the floor and lean back on their hands. Have them bend their knees, keeping their feet flat on the floor. Then have them lift their bottoms off the floor and try moving sideways like crabs do. Can they also move forward and backward?

We're Little Orange Crabs

Sung to: "The Farmer in the Dell"

We're little orange crabs
Who live down by the sea,
And wherever we do go
We're quick as quick can be.

We're little orange crabs
Who like to run and hide,
And when you see us walking by
It's always side to side.

Jean Warren

Children's Books:
- *Kermit the Hermit*, Bill Peet, (Houghton Mifflin, 1965).
- *Crab That Played With the Sea, A Just So Story*, Rudyard Kipling, (Bedrick, 1983).
- *House for Hermit Crab*, Eric Carle, (Picture Book Studio, 1987).

Contributors:
John M. Bittinger, Everett, WA
Wes Epperson, Placerville, CA
Ellen Javernick, Loveland, CO
Susan Peters, Upland, CA
Marie Wheeler, Tacoma, WA

DANDELIONS

Painting With Dandelions

Give each child a dandelion blossom and a piece of white paper. Set out small dishes of yellow tempera paint. Let the children use their dandelions as paint brushes to dab the yellow paint on their papers.

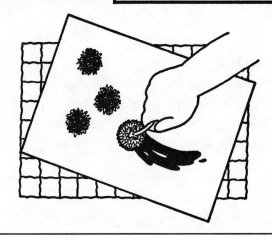

Dandelion Seed Pictures

Take the children outside to a place where there are many dandelions that have gone to seed. Give each child a piece of dark colored construction paper and a paint brush. Set out several shallow containers of glue. Let the children brush glue all over their papers. Then help the children hold their papers behind the dandelions while they blow the seeds onto them.

What's in a Name?

Show the children a dandelion with the flower, stem and leaves attached. Tell them that the word "dandelion" means "teeth of the lion" in French. Ask them to look at the dandelion leaves and see if they can guess how the dandelion got its name.

Dandelion Hunt

Take the children outside to a place where there are lots of dandelions. Have them go on a dandelion hunt. Ask them to find dandelions with big flowers. Then ask them to find ones with small flowers, ones with unopened flowers, ones with leaves, etc.

Dandelion Word Games

Have each child pick a dandelion that has gone to seed. Have the children hold the dandelions in front of their mouths. Encourage them to blow the seeds off their dandelions by saying words that begin with the "wh" sound, such as "why," "when" and "whisper." How many different words can they think of that start with that sound?

DANDELIONS

Dandy Lady

Sung to: "Mary Had a Little Lamb"

Once there was a dandy lady,
Dandy lady, dandy lady,
Once there was a dandy lady
Who loved to dance, they say.

She had beautiful hair of gold,
Hair of gold, hair of gold,
She had beautiful hair of gold
And loved to dance all day.

As time passed by and she grew old,
She grew old, she grew old,
As time passed by and she grew old
Her hair all turned to gray.

Now when the dandy lady dances,
Lady dances, lady dances,
Now when the dandy lady dances
Her hair all blows away.

Jean Warren

Dandelion Yellow

Paint a cardboard box yellow. Place the box in the middle of the room. Show the children yellow dandelions and talk about other things that are yellow. Then let the children find things in the room that are yellow and put them in the box.

Dandelion Eggs

Let the children help you pick some tender young dandelion leaves. (They taste best when picked before the plant has blossomed.) Wash the leaves, then dry them with paper towels. Have the children tear the leaves into bite-sized pieces. To make dandelion eggs, prepare scrambled eggs according to your usual recipe, adding the leaves just as the eggs are starting to set.

Children's Books:
- *Aminal*, Lorna Balian, (Abingdon, 1985).
- *Dandelion*, Barrie Watts, (Silver Burdett, 1987).

Mud Sculptures

Fill several dishpans with dirt and set them on a table. Have the children add water to the dirt to make mud. Then let them sculpt the mud into a variety of shapes. Ask the children what happens when they add more water. What happens when they add more dirt?

Mud Fingerpaint

Mix dirt and water in a big bowl to make mud. Put the mud on a table and let the children finger-paint with it. If desired, add glue to the mixture and have the children make handprints on a large piece of butcher paper.

Where Does Dirt Come From?

Explain to the children that dirt, or soil, is made from rocks, plants and animals. First, show them a rock and some sand. Tell them that after years and years of warming by the sun, freezing by the snow and ice and wearing away by the wind and rain, the rock eventually breaks into smaller and smaller pieces and becomes sand. Then show the children a sample of sand and a sample of dirt. Explain that dirt is sand that has tiny pieces of decaying plants and animals in it, which is why it looks and feels different from ordinary sand.

Dirt Safari

Go outside with the children. Spread a newspaper out on the grass and put two or three scoops of dirt on it. Give the children small sifters and magnifying glasses to use for examining the dirt. Can they see any parts of plants, animals or rocks in the dirt? What does the dirt look like? What does it feel and smell like?

DIRT

Dirt and Water

Fill a clear jar partway with dirt and water. Stir up the dirt and water and have the children observe what happens. Have them continue to watch the jar. What is happening now? Why is the dirt sinking to the bottom? What would happen if you stirred it up again?

Alike and Different

Find two different kinds of dirt and put them in separate jars. Ask the children to compare the two kinds of dirt. How are they alike? How are they different? Which dirt would be best for growing plants? Why?

"D" Sound

Fill a large dishpan with dirt. Bury a variety of objects in the dirt, including some objects whose names begin with "D," such as a toy dog, a pair of dice and a plastic duck. Have the children take turn digging through the dirt to find the objects whose names begin with "D."

I Love Dirt

Sung to: "Three Blind Mice"

I love dirt, I love dirt.
It can't hurt, on my shirt.
I love to squirt it with my hose,
I love to squish it with my toes,
The fun I have just grows and grows.
I love dirt.

Jean Warren

Children's Books:
- *The Real Hole,* Beverly Cleary, (Morrow, 1986).
- *The Carrot Seed,* Robert Krauss, (Harper, 1945).
- *Sun, the Wind and the Rain,* Lisa Peters, (Henry Holt, 1988).

Contributors:
Kristine Wagoner, Federal Way, WA

Dog Puppets

For each child cut a large triangle out of construction paper. Turn the triangle so that one of the points is facing down. Fold the top corners down to look like ears. Give each child one of the folded triangles. Have the children add facial features with felt-tip markers. Attach a Popsicle stick handle to each puppet.

Paw Prints

Make several dog paw-print stamps. For each stamp, cut a foot pad shape and four toe shapes out of corrugated cardboard. Glue the shapes in the correct positions to a wood block. Place folded paper towels in shallow containers and pour on small amounts of tempera paint. Let the children dip the stamps into the paint and use them to make paw prints all over pieces of construction paper.

Dog Tags

Let the children choose dog names for themselves. Write each child's chosen name on a construction paper bone shape. Have the children decorate their bone shapes with crayons. Attach yarn to the shapes and let the children wear them around their necks.

Dog Stories

Cut pictures of dogs out of magazines. Cover each picture with clear self-stick paper. Have the children sit in a circle and give each child a dog picture. Let the children take turns naming their dogs and telling stories about them. Encourage them by asking questions such as "What does your dog like to do? What color is your dog's fur? Where does your dog sleep? What does your dog like to eat? What tricks can your dog do?"

DOGS

Feeding the Dogs

Wash and dry five dog dishes. Number the dishes from 1 to 5 by taping numbered pieces of paper to the sides. Set out the dishes and fifteen dog biscuits. Let the children take turns identifying the numbers on the dishes and placing the appropriate number of biscuits in each one.

Variation: Instead of dog biscuits and dog dishes, use small bone shapes cut out of brown construction paper and paper bowls.

Find the Bone Game

Have the children sit in a circle. Select one child to be the Dog and have that child step outside. Hide a large soup bone (or a paper bone shape) in the room. Have the Dog return to the room and begin searching for his or her lost bone. As the Dog gets closer to the bone, have the rest of the children bark loudly. As the Dog gets farther away from the bone, have them bark very quietly. When the Dog has found the bone, let him or her select another child to be the new Dog.

There's a Doggy at the Door

Sung to: "If You're Happy and You Know It"

There's a doggy at the door,
   at the door,
There's a doggy at the door,
   at the door.
Oh, who could ask for more
Than a doggy at the door?
There's a doggy at the door,
   at the door.

There's a doggy in the house,
   in the house,
There's a doggy in the house,
   in the house.
Are you sure it's not a mouse?
No, a doggy in the house.
There's a doggy in the house,
   in the house.

There's a doggy on the stair,
   on the stair,
There's a doggy on the stair,
   on the stair.
Doesn't anybody care
That a doggy's on the stair?
There's a doggy on the stair,
   on the stair.

There's a doggy in the hall,
   in the hall,
There's a doggy in the hall,
   in the hall.
Well, he's playing with a ball,
The little doggy in the hall.
There's a doggy in the hall,
   in the hall.

There's a doggy in my room,
   in my room,
There's a doggy in my room,
   in my room.
Now he's chewing on a broom,
The little doggy in my room.
There's a doggy in my room,
   in my room.

There's a doggy on my bed,
   on my bed,
There's a doggy on my bed,
   on my bed.
Now he's licking at my head,
The little doggy on my bed.
There's a doggy on my bed,
   on my bed.

Scott Smith
Tacoma, WA

Pear Puppies

For each child place a lettuce leaf on a small plate. Put a pear half on top of the lettuce and add an apple wedge for an ear, a raisin for an eye, a mandarin orange segment for a dog collar and half a grape for a nose.

Doggy Bone Snacks

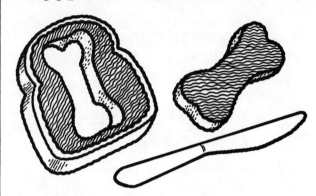

Spread slices of toast or bread with peanut butter. Cut the slices into bone shapes with a knife or a cookie cutter. Serve the "doggy bone" snacks to the children.

Dog Tricks

Have the children pretend to be dogs by crawling around on all fours. Encourage them to romp around and play like dogs and puppies. Then let one of the children pretend to be their trainer and ask them to do doggy tricks such as sit up, roll over, fetch (with their paws, instead of their mouths), play dead and beg.

My Puppy

As you recite the poem below, have the children pretend to be puppies and act out the movements described.

My puppy is quite amazing,
And tricks, he knows quite a few.
Here, let me show you my puppy
And some of the tricks he can do.

Puppy, puppy, watch when I say "Go!"
Puppy, puppy, wag your tail just so.
Wag, wag, wag, wag,
Wag your tail just so.

Puppy, puppy, watch when I say "Go!"
Puppy, puppy, roll your body just so.
Roll, roll, roll, roll,
Roll your body just so.

Puppy, puppy, watch when I say "Go!"
Puppy, puppy, jump up high just so.
Jump, jump, jump, jump,
Jump up high just so.

Additional verses: "Puppy, puppy, sniff your nose just so; Shake your paws just so; Sit up and beg just so."

Jean Warren

Children's Books:
- *Whistle for Willie*, Ezra Jacks Keats, (Viking, 1964).
- *Good Dog, Carl*, Alexandra Day, (Green Tiger, 1985).
- *Harry, the Dirty Dog*, Gene Zion, (Harper, 1956).

Contributors:
Sharon L. Olson, Minot, ND

Duck Finger Puppets

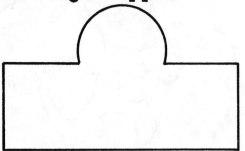

For each child cut a duck finger puppet shape, as shown above, out of white construction paper. Let the children glue cotton balls on their ducks. Cut eye shapes out of black construction paper and bill shapes out of orange construction paper. Have the children glue the eyes and bills on their duck shapes. Bend and tape the puppet tabs together to complete.

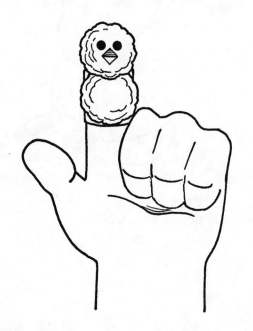

Paper Plate Duck Puppets

Give the children paper plates. Let them decorate the backs of their plates with felt-tip markers and orange construction paper bill shapes to create duck faces. Staple half of a paper plate over the front of each whole paper plate to create a pocket. Have the children put their hands in the pockets to make their puppets move.

Disappearing Ducks

Have the children pretend to be little ducks and line up behind you. Lead them around the room and have everyone recite the poem below. Begin the poem with the number of children playing. For six players, start the poem as follows:

Six little ducks went out to play
Over the hill and far away.
Mother Duck said, "Quack, Quack, Quack," (softly)
And five little ducks came waddling back.

As you waddle around the room, go behind a partition (a row of chairs, a table or a long piece of furniture). Have the child at the end of the line crouch down behind the partition while the other children continue to follow you. Keep repeating the poem, each time leaving a child behind. When all the children are behind the partition, change the last line of the poem to read: "And no little ducks came waddling back." Then recite the verse below and have all the children come waddling back out again.

No little ducks came out to play
Over the hill and far away.
Mother Duck said, "Quack, Quack, Quack!" (loudly)
And six little ducks came waddling back.

Jean Warren

The Little Ducklings

Have the children act out the movements described as you recite the following poem:

All the little ducklings
Line up in a row.
Quack, quack, quack,
And away they go.

They follow their mother
Waddling to and fro.
Quack, quack, quack,
And away they go.

Down to the big pond
Happy as can be.
Quack, quack, quack,
They are full of glee.

They jump in the water
And bob up and down.
Quack, quack, quack,
They swim all around.

All the little ducklings
Swimming far away.
Quack, quack, quack,
They'll play another day.

Elizabeth Vollrath
Stevens Point, WI

Dunk the Ducks

Fill a soft-sided inflatable wading pool with about 3 inches of water and put three or four plastic floating ducks in it. Then fill several squirt bottles with water. Invite the children to use the squirt bottles to "dunk the ducks."

Where's the Egg?

Have the children sit in a circle. Ask one child to be the Parent Duck and have the child leave the room. Hide a plastic "duck" egg somewhere in your room while the other children watch. Ask the Parent Duck to come back in and search for his or her egg. As the Parent Duck gets closer to the egg, have the other children quack loudly. As the Parent Duck gets farther away from the egg, have the children quack softly. When the egg has been found, choose another child to be the Parent Duck and start the game again.

Did You Ever See a Duck?

Sung to: "Did You Ever See a Lassie?"

Did you ever see a duck, a duck, a duck,
Did you ever see a duck who waddles so slow?
She waddles and waddles and waddles and waddles.
Did you ever see a duck who waddles so slow?

Did you ever see a duck, a duck, a duck,
Did you ever see a duck who quacks so fast?
She quacks and quacks and quacks and quacks.
Did you ever see a duck who quacks so fast?

Jean Warren

Ducks Like to Swim

Sung to: "My Bonnie Lies Over the Ocean"

Ducks like to swim in the water,
They stretch their webbed feet out in back.
Ducks sometimes swim in circles,
They swim and they swim and they quack.
Swim, swim, quack, quack,
They swim and they swim and they quack.
Swim, swim, quack, quack,
They swim and they swim and they quack.

Sue Brown
Louisville, KY

Children's Books:
- *Make Way for Ducklings,*
  Robert McCloskey, (Viking, 1941).
- *Runaway Duck,* David Lyon,
  (Lothrup, 1985).
- *Three Ducks Went Wandering,* Ron Roy,
  (Scholastic, 1980).

Contributors:
Betty Silkunas, Lansdale, PA
Elizabeth Vollrath, Stevens Point, WI

EGG CARTONS

Egg Carton Moon Scenes

Give each child a cardboard egg carton with a lid attached. Have the children paint the insides of their cartons and lids black or dark blue. Allow the paint to dry. Let the children create "moon creatures" by gluing plastic moving eyes on the cones between the cups in their cartons. Then let them glue silver stars and planet shapes cut from aluminum foil inside their lids to complete their moon scenes.

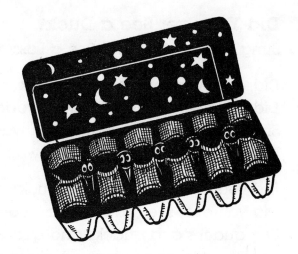

Collage Cartons

Prepare a collage carton for each child by filling the cups of an egg carton with materials such as dried beans, rice, popcorn kernels, pasta shapes, buttons, yarn, ribbon scraps and cotton balls. Give each child a carton and some glue. Help the children cut the lids off their cartons. Then let them glue their collage items on their lids.

Egg Cup Bluebells

Cut the egg cups out of cardboard egg cartons. Then cut the cups into bluebell shapes and let the children paint them blue. When the paint has dried, make stems by inserting the ends of green pipe cleaners through the bottoms of the bluebells, then bending the pipe cleaners into cane shapes. Let the children poke holes in the ends of precut green construction paper leaves and thread them on their bluebell stems.

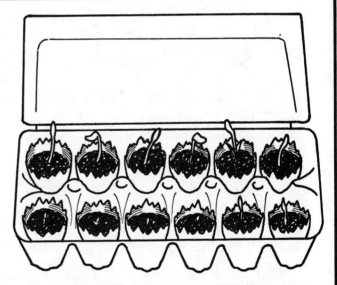

Variation: Cut the egg cups into tulip shapes and let the children paint them different colors.

Egg Carton Nursery

Place empty eggshell halves in the cups of an egg carton. Let the children fill the shells with potting soil and carefully plant one or two radish or carrot seeds in each one. Have them add a teaspoon of water to each shell. Keep the egg carton closed so that the seeds will stay warm and sprout more quickly. After the seeds have sprouted and grown into seedlings, have the children plant the eggshells outside, crushing them slightly before placing them in the ground.

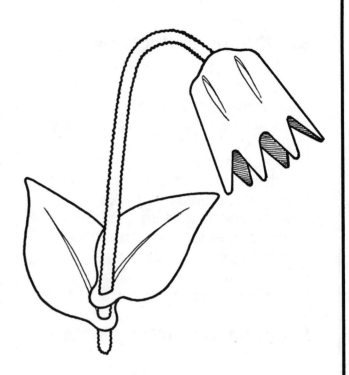

Variation: Let each child make an egg carton nursery of his or her own.

Egg Carton Collections

Give each child an egg carton before going on a nature walk. Encourage the children to put the treasures they find along the way in their cartons. When you return from your walk, have the children sort their collections by type of item, such as leaves, rocks or flowers. Then let them glue their items on pieces of construction paper or posterboard.

Egg Carton Number Game

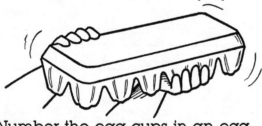

Number the egg cups in an egg carton from 1 to 12. Put a button in the carton and close the lid. Let the children take turns shaking the carton, opening the lid and identifying the number the button landed on.

Variation: Label the egg cups with colors or alphabet letters instead of numbers.

Egg Carton Memory Game

Place two or three different colored plastic eggs in an empty egg carton. Show the eggs to the children, then close the lid. Ask the children to name the colors of eggs they remember seeing. Open the lid to let them check their responses. Continue the game, adding a different colored egg each time.

Egg Carton Color Game

Collect twelve plastic eggs of various colors and a cardboard egg carton. Color the bottoms of the egg carton cups with felt-tip markers to match the colors of the eggs. Then let the children take turns placing the eggs in the matching colored egg cups.

Egg Carton Counter

Punch a hole in the bottom of each egg cup in an egg carton. Close the lid and turn the carton upside down so that the egg cups are facing up. Set out twelve clothespins. Let the children take turns putting one clothespin in the hole in each egg cup, counting as they go. Remove some of the clothespins and ask the children to count how many are left. Repeat, putting some clothespins in or taking some out each time.

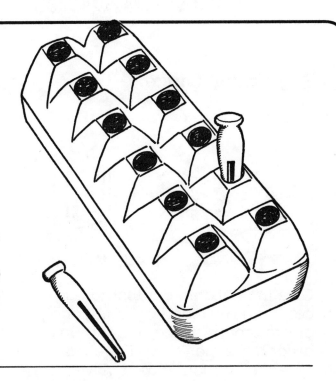

Color Sorting

Set out the bottom part of an egg carton, a small bowl of multi-colored popcorn kernels and a pair of tweezers. Let the children take turns using the tweezers to sort the popcorn kernels by color into the egg carton cups.

Variation: Instead of popcorn kernels, set out different colored cotton balls, pasta or buttons for the children to sort.

EGG CARTONS

Egg Carton Shakers

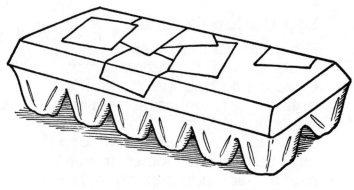

Give the children cardboard egg cartons. Have each child put one or two scoops of rice or beans in his or her carton. Help the children tape their cartons closed. Give them short crepe paper strips to glue all over their cartons. Allow the glue to dry. Then let the children use their egg carton shakers as rhythm instruments to accompany favorite songs. Or have them move their shakers as directed as you sing the song below.

Shake It

Sung to: "The Farmer in the Dell"

Shake your shaker high,
Shake your shaker low.
Shake it here and shake it there,
Now shake it by your toe.

Shake it back and forth,
Shake it round and round.
Shake it here and shake it there,
Now shake it up and down.

Gayle Bittinger

Egg Cup Puppets

Cut the egg cups out of cardboard egg cartons and give one to each child. Show the children how to use felt-tip markers to draw faces on the flat sides of their egg cups. Give the children small pieces of yarn to use for hair. Have them glue the yarn hair to their egg cups. Poke a pipe cleaner handle through the bottom of each egg cup puppet. Let the children use their puppets while singing songs or reciting familiar rhymes.

Snack Cartons

Set out a variety of bite-sized snack foods such as cheese cubes, grapes, raisins, cucumber chunks, carrot rounds, popcorn and peanuts. Give each child a Styrofoam egg carton that has been washed and dried. Have the children fill the egg cups in their cartons with the bite-sized foods. Then let them take their snack cartons outside for a picnic, if weather permits.

Children's Books:
- *Rechenka's Eggs,* Patricia Polacco, (Putnam, 1988).
- *Horton Hatches the Egg,* Dr. Seuss, (Random House, 1940).
- *Are You My Mother?,* P.D. Eastman, (Random House, 1966).

Contributors:
Sarah Cooper, Arlington, TX
Susan M. Paprocki, Northbrook, IL
Betty Silkunas, Lansdale, PA

Fabric Collages

Cut shapes of various sizes from different textured fabrics. Give the children pieces of construction paper. Let them glue the fabric shapes all over their papers. Then have the children rub their hands over their collages and describe the different textures they feel.

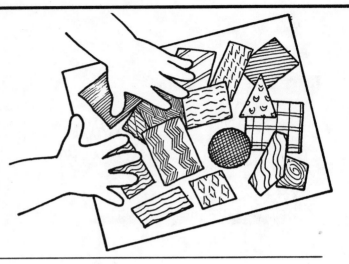

Fabric Placemats

For each child cut out a 12- by 18-inch rectangle of loosely woven fabric. Show the children how to unravel the edges of the fabric by carefully pulling out the threads from one direction. Have them unravel ½- to 1-inch rows around all the edges of their fabric pieces to make placemats. Then let the children use their placemats at snacktime or give them as gifts.

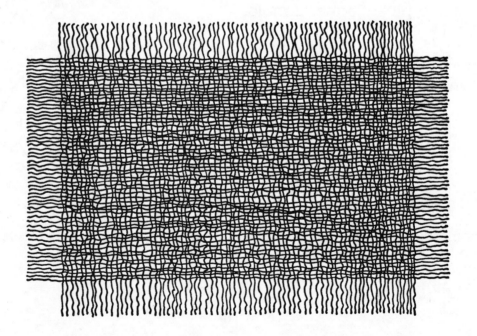

Fabric Directions Game

Give each child a large square piece of fabric. Have the children hold their squares and follow directions such as these: "Raise your squares high above your heads; Lower your squares to the floor; Place your squares in front of you; Put your squares behind you."

Fabric Color Game

Place various solid colors of fabric pieces on the floor. Ask the children to name the colors. Then have the children take turns finding objects in the room that match those colors. Have them place the objects on the matching colored pieces of fabric.

Fabric Square Match-Ups

Cut two squares each out of several different textured or patterned fabrics. Glue each square to an index card. Mix up the cards and place them on a table. Let the children take turns finding the matching fabric squares.

Clothesline Game

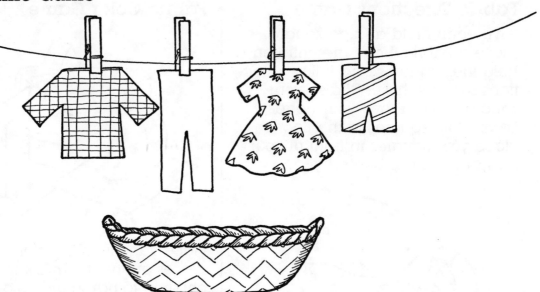

Hang a length of clothesline between two chairs and clip clothespins on the line. Cut clothing shapes out of fabric and place them in a basket. Then let the children take turns "hanging up the wash" as you give directions such as "Hang up the shirts; Hang up two pairs of pants; Hang up all the green clothes."

Fabric Feelie Bag

Cut small pieces out of different textured fabrics such as silk, cotton, wool, corduroy and burlap. Let the children feel the differences between the fabrics. Then put the fabric pieces in a bag. Let the children take turns putting their hands in the bag and guessing which fabrics they are touching before pulling them out.

Fabric Snack Packs

Have the children pack snacks such as fruit, raw vegetables and crackers in small squares of fabric. Help them tie the ends of the fabric together hobo-style. Then let the children carry their snack packs outside for a fun picnic.

Fabric Dancing

Give the children large fabric squares. Play recordings of music with dramatic differences in tempo, such as waltzes, marches, polkas and jazz. Have the children dance to the music while holding their fabric squares. Encourage them to wave, swirl, turn and sway their squares in time to the music.

Dramatic Play With Fabric

Have the children sit in a circle. Hold up large squares of fabric. Let the children try to think of different uses for the fabric squares. Then let them take turns using the squares for dramatic play. For example, they could pretend that the fabric pieces are hoods protecting them from a sudden rain shower. Or they could pretend that the squares are magic capes giving them super-

natural powers. Encourage the children to think of as many uses for the fabric squares as they can.

Children's Books:
- *Patchwork Quilt,* Valerie Flournoy, (Dial, 1985).
- *The Blanket That Had to Go,* Nancy E. Cooney, (Putnam, 1986).
- *Patchwork Cat,* William Mayne, (Knopf, 1983).

Contributors:
Carol Halpin, Allentown, PA

Feather Painting

Set out feathers or feather dusters and shallow containers of paint. Give each child a large construction paper bird shape. Let the children use the feathers as brushes to paint their birds. If the children are using single feathers, have them stick their feathers in the wet paint on their papers when they are done.

Painting Turkey Feathers

Cut a large turkey shape out of brown butcher paper and hang it on a wall or a bulletin board. Cut large turkey feather shapes out of construction paper. Pour several colors of tempera paint into shallow containers. Give the children real feathers and the feather shapes. Let them paint designs on their feather shapes with the real feathers. Attach the painted feather shapes to the turkey.

Feather Poem

Cut a turkey body shape out of brown felt and one feather shape each from the following colors of felt: red, blue, green, orange, yellow, purple, black, white and brown. Place the turkey shape on a flannelboard. As you recite the following poem, place the feathers on the turkey, one at a time.

Mr. Turkey was so sad,
He lost the feathers he once had.
Now he wants us to help him find
All the feathers of his kind.

We will look both high and low,
We will find them, don't you know.
Here's a red one and a blue,
Look, we've found a green one too.

Here's an orange one and a yellow,
Soon he'll be a feathered fellow.
Now we've found the purple one,
Black and white, we're almost done.

If we just look up and down,
I know we'll find the feather brown.
Now Mr. Turkey is so glad,
For we found the feathers he once had.

Gayle Bittinger

Feathers or Fur?

Explain to the children that birds have feathers on the outsides of their bodies while other animals have fur. Cut out magazine pictures of birds and other animals. Hold up the pictures, one at a time, and ask the children to tell you if feathers or fur cover the animal. What do the animals covered with feathers have in common?

Feather Dusting

Have the children sit in a circle. In the middle of the circle, place a chair and a feather duster. Have the children take turns using the duster to follow directions you give them, such as "Dust under the chair; Dust behind the chair; Dust the back of the chair; Dust the legs of the chair." Then have the children watch as you dust, and ask them to name the places you are dusting.

Found a Feather

Sung to: "Oh, My Darling Clementine"

Found a feather, found a feather,
Found a feather on the ground.
Oh, I am so very lucky
A feather to have found.

Picked it up, picked it up,
Picked it up just like that.
Picked up that pretty feather,
Then I put it in my hat.

Found a feather, found a feather,
Found a feather on the ground.
Oh, I am so very lucky
A feather to have found.

Jean Warren

Tail Feathers Game

For each child draw a picture of a bird (minus the tail) on a sheet of white construction paper. Use crayons to write numbers from 1 to 5 on the tail ends of the birds. Give each child five feather shapes cut out of colored construction paper. Number the feather shapes with sets of dots from 1 to 5. Then have the children glue the feathers over the corresponding numbers on their birds to make tails. Let them use crayons to color their bird bodies and add other details, if desired.

Colored Feather Game

Cut feather shapes out of selected colors of construction paper and place them in a paper bag. Have the children sit in a circle. Let one child at a time reach into the bag and take out a feather. Explain that in order to keep the feather, the child must name something that is a matching color (a red apple, a yellow banana, my blue shirt, etc.). Continue the game as long as desired, making sure that everyone ends up with the same number of feathers.

Children's Books:
- *Heather's Feathers*, Leatie Weiss, (Avon, 1978).
- *Bird's Nest*, Barrie Watts, (Silver Burdett, 1987).
- *Tico and Golden Wings*, Leo Lionni, (Knopf, 1987).

Contributors:
Nancy J. Heimark, Grand Forks, ND
Susan M. Paprocki, Northbrook, IL

Group Flag

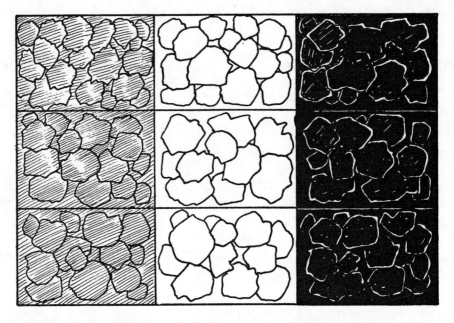

Set out three colors of construction paper and three matching colors of tissue paper. Let the children tear the tissue paper into small pieces and glue them all over the matching colored sheets of construction paper. Put the children's papers together on a wall or a bulletin board in the shape of a flag, arranging the colors in rows or columns to make stripes.

Personalized Flags

Explain to the children that every country has its own flag and that people often display or wave their flags on national holidays to honor their countries. Then set out various colors of self-stick dots, star stickers and pieces of vinyl tape. Give each child a sheet of construction paper. Let the children arrange the dots, stars and tape pieces on their papers to create their own flags.

Flag Time

Show the children an American flag or a picture of one. Ask the children to name places where they see the flag hanging. Have them name the colors on the flag. Together, count the white stripes, the red stripes and the stars.

Extension: Tell the children about Betsy Ross. It is said that she made America's first stars and stripes flag. It had thirteen stripes and thirteen stars. Have the children compare a picture of America's first flag with the flag flown today. How are the flags the same? How are they different?

Flag Match-Ups

Purchase a variety of small paper flags at a craft store. Divide the flags into matching pairs. Attach each of the flags to a small index card. Mix up the cards and let the children take turns finding the matching pairs of flags.

Flags in the Wind

Have the children pretend that they are flags hanging on flag poles and that the wind is blowing. Encourage them to move in various ways by asking questions such as "How would you move in a gentle breeze? How would you move in a storm? What would happen if the wind stopped suddenly?"

Flag Parade

Let the children carry their flags from the activity on page 80 in a Flag Parade. Sing the song below as the children march around the room.

Sung to: "When the Saints Go Marching In"

Oh, when the flags go marching by,
Oh, when the flags go marching by.
How we love to see all the colors,
When the flags go marching by.

Now here comes Jeff, and here comes Wayne,
And here comes Jamie and Shelley.
How we love to see all the colors
When the flags go marching by.

Repeat the second verse, substituting your children's names for the names in the song.

Jean Warren

The American Flag

Sung to: "Frere Jacques"

What is red? What is white?

What is blue? What is striped?

What has many stars?

What has many stars?

Can you guess how many there
      are?

Saundra Winnett
Lewisville, TX

Children's Books:
- *Fourth of July Story,* Alice Dalgliesh,
  (Macmillan, 1956).
- *Star-Spangled Banner,* Peter Spier,
  (Doubleday, 1973).

Graham Cracker Flags

Put small amounts of white frosting in three bowls. Add red food coloring to one bowl and blue food coloring to another. Let the children decorate graham crackers with the red, white and blue frosting to create "flags."

Variation: For a sugarless alternative, use whipped cream cheese and saltine crackers.

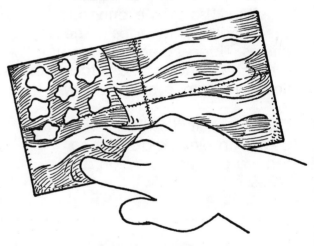

Contributors:
Joleen Meier, Marietta, GA

Flower Hangings

Cover a table with towels. Give each child two circles cut out of waxed paper. Place a variety of fresh flowers in the center of the table and let each child choose several to arrange on top of one of his or her waxed paper circles. Have each child cover his or her flowers with the second piece of waxed paper. Then place a towel on top of each child's waxed paper circles and press with a warm iron to seal the edges together. Use a hole punch to make holes at the tops of the circles. Thread pieces of yarn through the holes and arrange the flower hangings in a window.

Caution: Activities that involve the use of an electric appliance require adult supervision at all times.

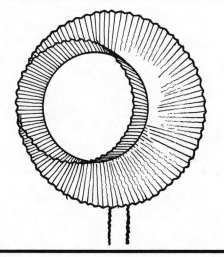

Daffodils

Give the children yellow and white paper baking cups. Have them each flatten one of the cups and spread glue on the center portion. Then have them each place a second cup upright on top of the glue to make a daffodil. If desired, let the children attach Popsicle sticks or pipe cleaners for stems.

Flower Jars

Let the children place small amounts of clay in baby food jar lids. Give them small dried flowers to arrange in the clay. Help the children screw the jars onto the lids. Tie ribbons around the necks of the jars and let the children give them as gifts.

Our Growing Garden

Cut petal shapes and circles out of various colors of construction paper. Give each child a circle and several petal shapes. Have the children glue their petal shapes to their circles. Let them draw faces on the circles, if desired. Measure each child and make a green construction paper stem that is the same length as the child's height. Write each child's name length-wise on his or her stem. Attach the stems to a wall or a bulletin board. Add the children's flowers to their stems. Cut leaf shapes out of green construction paper and attach them to the stems. Title the display ''Our Growing Garden'' or ''The Kinder Garden.'' If desired, measure the children every few months and add to the lengths of the stems.

FLOWERS

Flower Box

Cut flower shapes out of various colors of construction paper. Let the children glue them to Popsicle sticks. Fill a shallow box with dirt or sand. Have the children "plant" the flowers in the dirt in rows of twos, threes or fours. Encourage them to plant the rows from left to right or from back to front. Or direct the children to plant a red flower in front of a yellow flower, an orange flower behind a blue flower, etc.

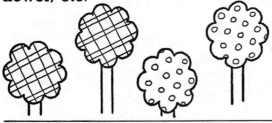

Flower Match-Ups

Cut ten identical flower shapes from construction paper and group them in pairs. Glue a different kind of fabric to each pair of flowers. Mix up the flowers and let the children take turns finding the matching pairs.

Variation: Cut pairs of identical flower shapes from five different colors of construction paper. Let the children take turns finding the flowers with matching colors.

Four Little Flowers

Cut four flower shapes out of felt and place them on a flannelboard. Let the children take turns removing the flowers as you recite the following poem:

Four little flowers
I did see.
I picked one,
Then there were three.

Three little flowers,
Pretty and new.
I picked another,
Then there were two.

Two little flowers
Out in the sun.
I picked one more,
Then there was one.

One little flower
Left in the sun.
I picked it too,
Then there were none.

Jean Warren

Flowers Are Blooming
Sung to: "Frere Jacques"

Flowers are blooming,
Flowers are blooming,
All around, all around.
All the pretty colors,
All the pretty colors
On the ground, on the ground.

Let's go see them,
Let's go see them,
Blooming bright, blooming bright.
Use your nose to smell them,
Use your eyes to see them.
What a sight! What a sight!

Sharon Clendenen
Syracuse, NY

In Our Springtime Garden
Sung to: "The Mulberry Bush"

What a lovely time of year,
Time of year, time of year.
What a lovely time of year
In our springtime garden.

See the flowers swing and sway,
Swing and sway, swing and sway.
See the flowers swing and sway
In our springtime garden.

Jean Warren

Children's Books:
• *A Reason for a Flower,* Ruth Heller, (Putnam, 1983).
• *Rose in My Garden,* Arnold Lobel, (Scholastic, 1985).
• *Miss Rumphius,* Barbara Cooney, (Viking, 1982).

Contributors:
Betty Ruth Baker, Waco, TX
Kristine Wagoner, Federal Way, WA

FROGS

Frog Fingerpainting

Cut large lily pad shapes out of butcher paper. Give each child one of the shapes with a small amount of green fingerpaint on it. Let the children pretend that their hands are frogs hopping here and there as they spread the paint across their lily pads.

Frog Puppets

Give each child two cotton balls and the following shapes cut out of construction paper: a large green circle, two small black circles, four green strips and a red tongue. Have each child fold his or her green circle in half and glue the cotton balls near the fold. Have the children glue their small black circles on the cotton balls to make eyes. Then have them glue their green strips to their folded circles for legs. Let them complete their puppets by gluing their red tongue shapes inside their folded circles.

Five Little Frogs

Recite the poem below with the children, letting them fill in the blanks. At the end of the poem, ask them to name places they think the frogs might have gone.

Five little frogs
Were down at the pond,
Down at the pond at play.
Along came a hungry _____,
And chased one frog away.

Four little frogs
Were down at the pond,
Down at the pond at play.
Along came a wiggly _____,
And chased one frog away.

Three little frogs
Were down at the pond,
Down at the pond at play.
Along came a giant _____,
And chased one frog away.

Two little frogs
Were down at the pond,
Down at the pond at play.
Along came a purple _____,
And chased one frog away.

One little frog
Was down at the pond,
Down at the pond at play.
Along came a flying _____,
And chased the frog away.

Then no little frogs
Were down at the pond,
Down at the pond at play.
Where do you think the little frogs
    went
When they all hopped away?

Sue Foster
Mukilteo, WA

Frog Jump

Let the children pretend to be frogs. Have them squat down with their arms straight out in front of them. Then have them jump forward, raising their arms high into the air before returning to a squatting position. Ask them to jump fast, to take big frog jumps, to take a certain number of jumps, to jump slowly and to take little frog jumps.

Little Green Frogs

Have the children pretend to be little green frogs crouched down in the grass. Then recite the rhyme below and have the children take big "frog hops" every time they hear the word "hop." When they hear the word "stop," have them stay crouched down without moving. Repeat the rhyme, changing a different "hop" to "stop."

Little green frog, won't you
Hop – hop – hop?
Little green frog, won't you
Hop – hop – stop?

Jean Woods
Tulsa, OK

Frog Skin

Explain to the children that some types of frogs change their skin color from light to dark green depending on where they are. For example, when this type of frog sits on a white rock it will have skin that is a lighter shade of green than when it sits on a dark green leaf. Ask the children why they think that the frogs might do this.

Extension: At a paint store pick up a paint chip card for the color green. Cut out the individual color chips and mount them on index cards. Let the children take turns arranging the chips from light to dark.

Listen to the Frog

Sung to: "Three Blind Mice"

Listen to the frog, listen to the frog,
Croaking on a log, croaking on a log.
He croaks about this and he croaks about that,
I find his croaking a tad bit flat,
It's very clear that he needs to chat.
Quiet down, frog!

Susan M. Paprocki
Northbrook, IL

The Frog Lives in the Pond

Sung to: "The Farmer in the Dell"

The frog lives in the pond,
Her tongue is oh, so long.
It reaches high to catch a fly.
The frog lives in the pond.

Jean Warren

Children's Books:
- *Jump, Frog, Jump!*, Robert Kalan,
  (Scholastic, 1981).
- *Princess and the Frog*, A. Vissey,
  (Little Brown, 1985).
- *Frog Prince*, Brothers Grimm,
  (Troll, 1979).

Contributors:
Sharon L. Olson, Minot, ND

Greeting Card Rubbings

Collect a variety of greeting cards with raised designs. Set out the cards and some crayons. Let the children each select a card and staple a piece of typing paper over it. Have the children rub crayons across their papers until the raised designs show through.

Sewing Cards

Use a hole punch to punch holes around the edges of greeting cards. On each card tie one end of a piece of yarn through one of the holes. Then wrap the other end of the yarn with tape to make a "needle." Give each child one of the cards to sew around.

Greeting Card Puppets

Find greeting cards with pictures of animals, people or other characters on them. Cut the characters out and attach each one to a Popsicle stick handle. Let the children choose puppets to hold. Then lead them in a group discussion while they pretend to be their puppet characters.

Greeting Card Story

Place several greeting cards in a box. Have the children sit in a circle. Have one child reach into the box and pull out a card. Use the picture on the card to begin your greeting card story. Let the children take turns pulling out greeting cards. As they do so, incorporate each picture into the story.

GREETING CARDS

Animal Cards

Collect an assortment of greeting cards with pictures of animals on them. Lay the greeting cards face down on a table. Ask the children, one at a time, to turn over a card and identify the animal pictured on it. Then ask the rest of the children questions such as "Where does this animal live? What would you do if you were this animal? What sound does it make?"

Matching Cards

Collect matching pairs of holiday greeting cards, illustrated note cards or party invitations. Mix up the cards and let the children take turns finding the ones that match.

Variation: Cut all the cards to the same size and let the children play Concentration with them.

Puzzle Cards

Cut greeting cards into puzzle pieces (vary the size and number of pieces according to the children's abilities). Put each puzzle in a recloseable plastic bag. Let the children select puzzles, put them together, then put the pieces back into the bags.

Music Cards

Collect several greeting cards and write the words to favorite songs on the backs. Ask a child to select a card. Then have everyone sing the song that is written on the back of it. Continue until all of the music cards have been chosen.

Children's Books:
- *Post Office Book,* Gail Gibbons, (Harper, 1982).
- *Your Best Friend, Kate,* Pat Brisson, (Macmillan, 1989).
- *The Jolly Postman,* Allan Ahlberg, (Little Brown, 1986).

Contributors:
Pat Cook, Hartford, VT

Horseshoe Prints

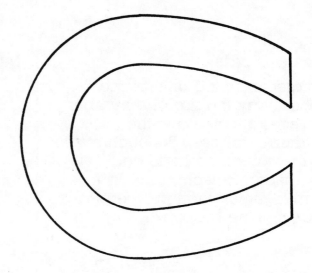

Make horseshoe stamps by cutting sponges into horseshoe shapes. For paint pads, fold paper towels in half, place them in shallow containers and add small amounts of tempera paint. Give the children large pieces of paper. Let them press the horseshoe stamps on the paint pads and then on their papers to make horseshoe prints. Encourage them to make prints as if they were horses galloping or trotting along.

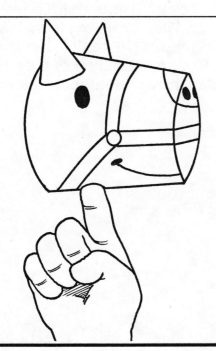

Horse Puppet

Make a hole large enough for a finger in the side of a paper or Styrofoam cup. Lay the cup on its side with the hole down. Glue ear shapes cut from construction paper on top of the cup and add pieces of ribbon for a bridle. Use felt-tip markers to add eyes, a nose and a mouth. Place the puppet on your finger and let the puppet talk about horses. Encourage the children to ask the puppet questions.

Horse Color Game

Cut five horse body shapes of white posterboard. Paint each shape a different color. Paint two spring-type clothespins to match each of the shapes. Allow the paint to dry. Set out the horse body shapes and the clothespin "horse legs." Have the children clip the matching colored clothespins on each body shape to complete the horses.

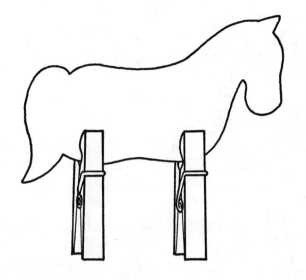

Hobby Horses

Make simple hobby horses by stuffing any kind of socks (except tube socks) with cloth or newspaper and fastening them around the ends of yardsticks with rubber bands. If desired, add button eyes and yarn manes. Let the children ride the hobby horses outside or around the room.

Lasso the Horse

Make large rings out of rope or clothesline. Place a rocking horse in the center of the room. Let the children take turns trying to "lasso" the horse by tossing the rings over its head.

Variation: If a rocking horse is unavailable, use a chair or an upside-down waste basket.

Little Horsey

Sung to: "Frere Jacques"

Little horsey, little horsey,
By a stream, by a stream.
The horsey's drinking water,
The horsey's drinking water.
Slurp, slurp, slurp; slurp, slurp, slurp.

Little horsey, little horsey,
Running fast, running fast.
The horsey's running this way,
The horsey's running that way.
Clip, clip, clop; clip, clip, clop.

G.S. Long
Mertztown, PA

Clippity, Clippity, Clop

Sung to: "Hickory Dickory Dock"

Clippity, clippity, clop,
The horses go clip, clop.
They gallop and gallop,
They start and they stop.
Clippity, clippity, clop.

Sue Brown
Louisville, KY

Feeding Time

Horses enjoy snacking on apples and carrots. For a special "horsey treat" serve the children sliced apples and carrot sticks.

Children's Books:
- *Good Night, Horsey,* Frank Asch, (Prentice Hall, 1981).
- *Fritz and the Beautiful Horses,* Jan Brett, (Houghton Mifflin, 1981).
- *The Girl Who Loved Wild Horses,* Paul Goble, (Bradbury, 1978).

Ice Sculpture

Place a block of ice in a dishpan. Put a small bowl of rock salt and a spoon close by. Let the children take turns spooning the salt on the ice. Wherever the rock salt touches the ice, the ice will melt faster, leaving a pattern of holes. In addition, set out three eyedroppers and three small containers filled with diluted red, yellow and blue food coloring. Let the children drop the colors on the ice. As the ice melts, the colors will run together and produce secondary colors.

Ice Painting

Give each child a piece of construction paper and an ice cube. Sprinkle a small amount of powder tempera paint on each child's paper. Have the children rub their ice cubes over the powder tempera. As the ice melts, it will turn the powder into liquid paint that dries quickly on their papers.

Extension: While doing this activity, let the children try on mittens to feel how wearing them protects their hands from the cold.

Ice Cube Magic

Place an ice cube in a glass of cold water. Ask the children if they can think of any way to lift the ice cube out of the water without touching it. Accept all of their answers, then show them this trick. Soak a piece of thread in cold water. Lay the thread on top of the ice cube and sprinkle the ice cube and the thread with salt. Ask the children to help you count to ten. Then carefully lift up the string; the ice cube is now attached to it.

Melting Ice

Fill paper cups partway with water and freeze. Give each of the children a cup of ice and have them put their cups in different places around the room. Have them check their cups every 5 to 10 minutes to see how their ice is melting. Which cup of ice melted first? Which melted last? Why? What would make the ice melt slower? Faster?

What Is Cold?

Have the children sit in a circle. Give one child an ice cube. Have him or her name something else that is cold before passing the ice cube to the next child. Continue until each child has had a chance to hold the ice cube and name something cold.

Insulation Experiment

Set out a bowl of ice cubes and a variety of insulation materials such as tissue paper, aluminum foil, plastic wrap, fabric and newspaper. Let the children wrap each ice cube in a different material. Place each insulated ice cube and one bare ice cube in separate bowls. After about an hour, have the children carefully unwrap the ice cubes and compare them to the bare ice cube. Which ice cube melted the most? The least? Which insulation material worked best?

Ice Cube Colors

Tint water with food coloring and freeze to make one tray of red ice cubes, one tray of yellow and one tray of blue. Place three clear plastic glasses on a table and put a different colored ice cube into each glass. Periodically, have the children observe as the ice changes to colored water. Then place a red ice cube and a yellow ice cube together in another glass and have the children observe as the ice melts and creates orange. Repeat the process, using a blue and a yellow ice cube to make green and a red and a blue ice cube to make purple. Then let the children use the remaining colored ice cubes to set up their own color experiments.

Counting Ice Cubes

Use a permanent felt-tip marker to number five paper cups from 1 to 5 and set out fifteen ice cubes. Let the children take turns using ice tongs to put the appropriate number of ice cubes in each cup.

Icicles

Let the children pretend to be icicles. As you recite the poem below, have them "melt" until they end up in "puddles" on the floor.

I'm a frozen icicle, hanging in the sun.

First I start to melt,

Then I start to run.

Drip, drip, drip, drip,

Melting can be fun.

Donna Mullenix
Thousand Oaks, CA

Ice Skating

Make an imaginary pond for the children to ice skate on by outlining an area in your room with yarn. Make benches by putting sets of two or three chairs together. Let the children sit on the benches and pretend to put on their skates. Then have them step onto the pond to skate and step off to rest or remove their skates. Accompany the skating with music, if desired.

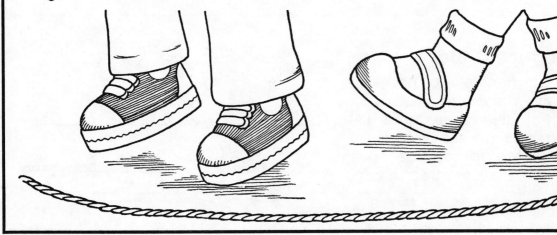

I'm a Little Ice Cube

Sung to: "I'm a Little Teapot"

I'm a little ice cube, frosty and square.
I make things icy cold everywhere.
If it gets too warm, I better watch out,
'Cause I will melt, there is no doubt.

Gayle Bittinger

Warm and Cold Snacks

Pour small amounts of warm juice into cups. Give each child a cup and ask him or her to taste the juice. Then give the children ice cubes to place in their cups. Have them taste the juice again. What has happened to the juice? What is happening to the ice cubes? Which taste did the children like best? If desired, serve chilled and non-chilled apple slices or carrot sticks for the children to compare as well.

Children's Books:
- *Snowy Day*, Ezra Jack Keats, (Viking, 1962).
- *David and the Ice Elf*, Winifred Morris, (Macmillan, 1988).
- *Icebergs and Glaciers*, Semour Simon, (Morrow, 1987).

Contributors:
John M. Bittinger, Everett, WA
Elizabeth Lokensgard, Appleton, WI
Donna Mullenix, Thousand Oaks, CA
Kay Roozen, Des Moines, IA

Jar Paperweights

Pour table salt into several bowls and add a different color of powder tempera paint to each one. Stir well. Let the children spoon the different colors of salt into baby food jars, creating patterns by layering the colors. Be sure the jars are filled completely. Spray paint the jar lids silver or gold. Spread glue around each child's jar rim and screw a spray-painted lid on tightly.

Variation: Use sand instead of salt.

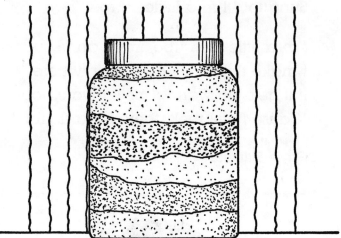

Popcorn Jars

Give each child a baby food jar and a jar lid. Let the children glue pieces of popped popcorn on top of their lids. When the glue has dried, brush one or two coats of clear varnish over the popcorn. Allow the varnish to dry. If desired, let the children put popcorn kernels in their jars before screwing on their decorated lids.

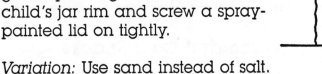

Mixing Jar

Fill a jar part way with water and part way with oil, leaving some space below the rim. Secure the lid tightly and shake. What happens to the oil and water? Add a few drops of food coloring. Now what happens when you shake the jar? When you turn the jar upside down?

Fizzing Jar

Fill a jar with water and put in three or four popcorn kernels. Add a fizzing antacid tablet. Have the children observe as the popcorn kernels begin to "dance" in the fizzing, bubbling water.

Science Jars

Fill identical jars with different materials such as sand, water, dirt, salt, popcorn kernels, cotton balls, rice, rocks and water. Let the children hold and shake the jars. Which jars are the lightest? Which are the heaviest? Which ones make sounds when they are shaken? What kinds of sounds?

Jar Planters

Have the children each choose a jar to use for a planter. Give them permanent felt-tip markers and let them carefully use the markers to decorate the sides of their jars. Then have the children spoon dirt into their jars and plant seeds in them.

Colored Crystal Jars

For each child mix 1 tablespoon Epsom salts and 1 tablespoon water in a baby food jar. Then stir in ¼ teaspoon of red, blue or green food coloring. Over the next few days have the children observe what happens as the water in their jars evaporates and small crystals begin to form. Keep a magnifying glass on hand for closer examination.

Color Mixing Experiment

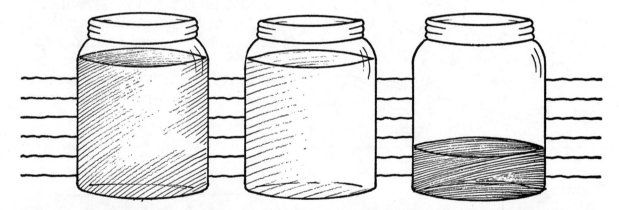

Place three jars on a table. Fill two of the jars with water and leave the third jar empty. Use food coloring to color the water in one of the jars red and the water in the other jar blue. Place an eyedropper in each jar of water. Then let the children take turns using the eyedroppers to squeeze drops of red and blue water into the empty jar to create purple.

Variation: Color the water in the jars red and yellow for making orange, or yellow and blue for making green.

Directions Game

Have the children sit in a circle and give each one a small jar. Give the children directions for moving their jars, such as "Put your jar behind you; Place your jar in your lap; Hold your jar on top of your head." Then let the children take turns giving one other directions.

Jar Lid Matching Game

Collect several different sizes of jar lids. On the inside of a file folder, make prints by dipping the rim of each lid into paint and pressing it on the folder. Clean the paint off the lids and allow the paint on the folder to dry. Then let the children take turns placing the jar lids on top of the matching prints.

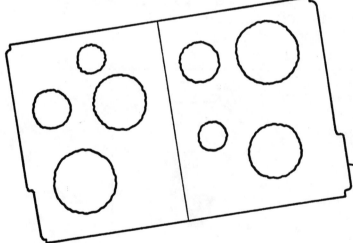

JARS

Sizing Up Jars

Find five or six jars of varying sizes. Set out the jars and let the children take turns arranging them from smallest to largest.

Color Game

Tape a different colored piece of construction paper on each of several jars. Cut pictures of matching colored objects out of magazines. Cover the pictures with clear self-stick paper for durability, if desired. Have the children take turns selecting a picture, identifying its color and placing it in the appropriate jar.

"J" Jar

Tape the letter "J" to the outside of a large jar placed on a table. Next to the jar place a variety of items whose names begin with "J," such as a jelly bean, a jack, a small plastic jack-o'-lantern, a toy jet, a toy jeep and a jingle bell. Then place next to those items a variety of objects whose names begin with other letters, such as a button, a crayon, a pencil, a key, a rock and a spoon. Have the children put the items whose names begin with "J" in the jar.

Musical Jars

Fill five jars with different amounts of water. Let the children take turns tapping the jars with a spoon. Which jar makes the highest sound? Which makes the lowest sound? Talk about how the amounts of water in the jars affect the sounds they make. Then have the children arrange the jars in order from lowest to highest sounds.

Snacks From Jars

At snacktime serve the children a variety of foods that come in jars, such as peanut butter (spread on crackers), pickles, applesauce and juice.

Children's Books:
• *A Chair for My Mother,* Vera Williams, (Greenwillow, 1982).

Contributors:
Marion Bergstrom, Kent, WA
Valerie Bielsker, Lenexa, KS
Karen L. Brown, Siloam Springs, AR
Marjorie Debowy, Stony Brook, NY
Annette Delaney, Houston, TX
Barbara Robinson, Glendale, AZ

Kite Mural

Give each child a kite shape that has been cut out of construction paper and folded in half lengthwise. Let the children unfold their shapes and use eye droppers to squeeze drops of tempera paint on one side of their papers. Then have them refold their shapes and rub their hands gently across the tops. Let them open up their kite shapes to reveal the designs they have made. Tape pieces of yarn to the shapes for kite strings. Attach the kite shapes to blue butcher paper that has been hung on a wall or a bulletin board. If desired, fluff out several cotton balls and glue them on the butcher paper for clouds. Construction paper bird shapes can also be added to complete the mural.

Fly a Kite

Purchase an inexpensive kite. Take the children and the kite outside on a windy day. Let them take turns helping you fly the kite. What happens when they let out the string? When they take in the string? When the wind stops blowing?

Kite Friends

Cut five kite shapes out of felt. Add yarn tails that have felt bow shapes attached, if desired. Place the kites on a flannelboard, one at a time, as you recite the following poem:

One little kite in the sky so blue,
Along came another, then there were two.

Two little kites flying high above me,
Along came another, then there were three.

Three little kites, just watch how they soar,
Along came another, then there were four.

Four little kites, so high and so alive,
Along came another, then there were five.

Five little kites dancing 'cross the sky,
What a sight to see, way up so high!

Jean Warren

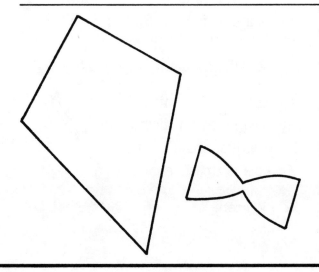

Color Kites

Cut kite and bow shapes out of five different colors of felt. Attach a yarn tail to each kite shape. Place the kite shapes on a flannelboard and put the bow shapes in a pile in nearby. Have the children identify the colors of the bows and place them on the tails of the matching colored kites.

Kite Puzzles

Cut ten kite shapes out of different patterned wallpaper samples. Cover the shapes with clear self-stick paper for durability, if desired. Cut each kite shape in half lengthwise. Mix up the halves and let the children take turns putting the kites back together.

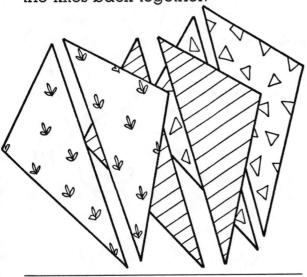

Kite Flying

Have the children pair up. In each pair have one child pretend to be the kite and the other child pretend to be the kite flyer. Have the kite flyers reel out their kites and move them up and down and back and forth. Then have them reel in their kites and trade places with their partners.

My Kite

Sung to: "The Farmer in the Dell"

My kite is up so high,
My kite is up so high.
Oh my, just watch it fly,
My kite is up so high.

My kite is falling down,
My kite is falling down.
Oh no, it's down so low,
My kite is falling down.

The wind has caught my kite,
The wind has caught my kite.
What fun, I'm on the run,
The wind has caught my kite.

My kite is up so high,
My kite is up so high.
Oh my, just watch it fly,
My kite is up so high.

Jean Warren

I Like Kites

Sung to: "Three Blind Mice"

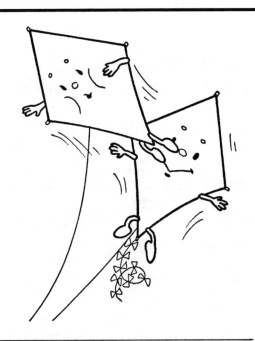

I like kites, I like kites.
They fly high, they fly high.
They keep on spinning round and round,
Sometimes they even touch the ground,
They fly through the air without a sound.
Oh, I like kites!

Linda Osmun
Bloomfield, NJ

Kite Sandwiches

Give the children bread and cheese slices that have been cut into kite shapes. Let them put their slices together to make kite sandwiches.

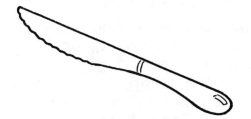

Children's Books:
- *Curious George Flies a Kite*, Margaret Rey, (Houghton Mifflin, 1958).
- *Emperor and the Kite*, Jane Yolen, (Putnam, 1988).

Ladybug Paperweights

Take the children on a walk to find ladybug-shaped rocks. Have the children paint their rocks red. Allow the paint to dry. Let each child use a black felt-tip marker to draw a line and several dots on his or her painted rock. Glue felt to the bottoms of the ladybug paper-weights, if desired.

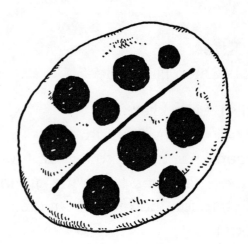

Ladybug Prints

Have the children press their thumbs on red stamp pads and make thumbprints on pieces of white paper. Then let them turn their thumbprints into ladybugs by adding dots and six legs to each one with black felt-tip markers.

Ladybug Life Cycle

Just like the butterfly and many other insects, the ladybug goes through four distinct stages of development. This process is called "metamorphosis." The stages are the egg, the larva, the pupa and the adult. Have the children act out the stages of the ladybug's life by pretending to be eggs on the leaf of a plant; hungry larvae crawling everywhere and eating everything in sight; pupae lying perfectly still on branches or leaves as the wings, legs and antennae of adult ladybugs are formed; then adult ladybugs spreading their wings to dry before flying away to find food.

Ladybug Puzzle Game

Cut large ladybug shapes out of red posterboard, one for every two children. Attach black self-stick circles to each shape. Cut each shape into two puzzle pieces. Mix up all of the pieces and give one to each child. Then have the children move around the room and try to find their "puzzle partners" by matching up their puzzle pieces. When all the ladybug puzzles have been put together, mix up the pieces and play the game again.

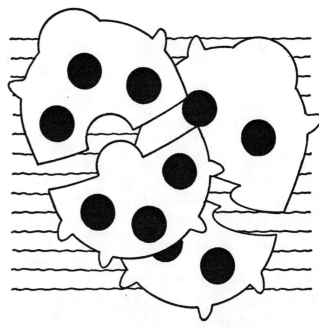

Ladybug Number Books

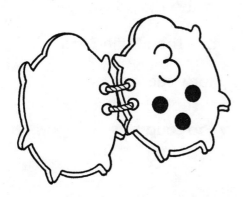

For each child cut five large ladybug shapes out of red construction paper. Put the shapes together, punch two holes on the left-hand side and tie with yarn to make a book. Use a black felt-tip marker to number the pages from 1 to 5.

Give a book and fifteen black self-stick circles to each child. Help the children put the appropriate numbers of black circles on their pages according to the numbers written on them.

Ladybug Matching

Draw a ladybug shape on each of ten index cards and divide the cards into pairs. Mark each pair of ladybugs with a different number of spots. Mix up the cards and let the children take turns counting the spots on the ladybugs to find the matching pairs.

Lucky Ladybug

Cut a large ladybug shape out of red felt and several ladybug spots out of black felt. Place the ladybug shape on a flannelboard. Sing the song with the children and ask a child to put two felt spots on the ladybug shape. Take the spots off and sing the song again, this time naming a different number of spots. Ask another child to add that many spots to the ladybug shape. Repeat the song until each child has had a chance to put spots on the ladybug.

Sung to: "The Muffin Man"

Lucky ladybug has two spots,
Has two spots, has two spots.
Lucky ladybug has two spots,
Lucky ladybug.

Sue Foster
Mukilteo, WA

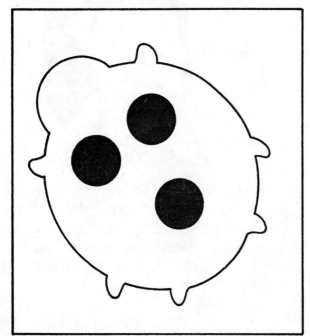

Little Red Bug

Cut a ladybug shape out of red felt and five ladybug spots out of black felt. Place the ladybug shape on a flannelboard. As you read the poem below, add the black spots, one at a time.

Little red bug, oh so cute,
Here's a black spot for your suit.
Now you go and have some fun
With your spot, your very first one.

Little red bug, oh so cute,
Here's a black spot for your suit.
It's so nice to own a few,
So enjoy these lovely two.

Little red bug, oh so cute,
Here's a black spot for your suit.
We are very pleased to see
How you look with all three.

Little red bug, oh so cute,
Here's a black spot for your suit.
You might feel that you need more,
So we proudly give you four.

Little red bug, oh so cute,
Here's a black spot for your suit.
Heaven, heaven sakes alive,
Look at you, you're wearing five!

Susan M. Paprocki
Northbrook, IL

Ladybug Treat

Add yellow and red food coloring to whipped cream cheese. Spread the orange-colored cheese on oval crackers. Add several raisins to each cracker for ladybug spots.

I'm a Little Ladybug

Sung to: "I'm a Little Teapot"

I'm a little ladybug on the go,
Landing on an arm, now an elbow.
See me fly around and around your hand,
Now watch as on your thumb I land.

I'm a little ladybug searching for some toes,
But watch me quickly land on your nose.
Now I look around and head for your hair,
I muss it up a bit, then pat it down with care.

I'm a little ladybug looking for a knee,
I'm just so happy you're not bugged by me.
Now you see me heading for your chest,
This little ladybug needs some rest.

Have the children use their fingers as "ladybugs" to act out the movements described suggested in the song.

Susan M. Paprocki
Northbrook, IL

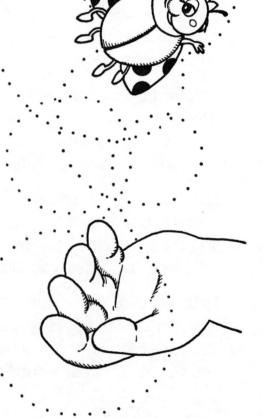

Found a Ladybug

Sung to: "Oh, My Darling
    Clementine"

Found a ladybug, found a ladybug,
Found a ladybug just now.
Just now I found a ladybug,
Found a ladybug just now.

It was red, it was red,
It was red just now.
It was red with black spots,
Red with black spots just now.

Betty Silkunas
Lansdale, PA

See the Ladybug

Sung to: "Frere Jacques"

See the ladybug, see the ladybug,
Watch it crawl, watch it crawl.
See it crawling higher,
See it crawling higher.
Watch it crawl, up the wall.

See the ladybug, see the ladybug,
Watch it crawl, watch it crawl.
See it crawling lower,
See it crawling lower.
Way down low, to my toe.

Jean Warren

Children's Books:
- *Grouchy Ladybug*, Eric Carle,
  (Harper, 1977).
- *Ladybug, Ladybug*, Ruth Brown,
  (Dutton, 1988).

Contributors:
Sue Foster, Mukilteo, WA
Susan M. Paprocki, Northbrook, IL

Magnetic Art

Cut a variety of shapes out of colorful pieces of posterboard. Cut self-stick magnetic strips into small squares and attach one to the back of each shape. (Self-stick magnetic strips are available at craft and variety stores.) Set out the shapes and several cookie sheets. Let the children arrange the shapes on the cookie sheets to create designs.

Clay Hand Magnets

Combine a 1-pound box of baking soda with 1 cup cornstarch in a saucepan. Gradually add 1¼ cup water and stir until smooth. Cook over medium heat, stirring constantly, until the mixture is thick and dough-like. Knead the clay on a tabletop and then flatten. Trace around each child's hand on the clay. Cut out the hand shapes and allow the clay to dry overnight. Let the children decorate their hand shapes with various colors of tempera paint. Have them sprinkle on glitter while the paint is still wet, if desired. Use strong glue to attach two small magnets to the back of each hand shape.

Magnetic Exploration

Have the children sit in a circle and give them each a magnet. Tell them that magnets stick to some things but not to others. Show them how a magnet sticks to a paper clip. Give them each a paper clip and let them feel the pull of their magnets on them. Next have them try to stick their magnets to their clothes. There is no pull, so the magnets will not stick. Then let them explore the room with their magnets, finding things that their magnets will stick to and things that they won't. How are the things that magnets stick to alike? (They are made of iron or steel.)

Magnet Magic

Fill a jar with water and place a paper clip in it. Make the paper clip dance up and down in the water by moving a magnet up and down the outside of the jar. The paper clip moves because the magnetic force passes through the glass and the water to the paper clip.

Magnetic Attraction

Let the children discover that magnets can attract or repel each other by experimenting with donut-shaped magnets and small sections of dowels set in playdough bases. Have the children try putting the magnets on the dowels so that they stick together. Then have them try to put them on the dowels so that the magnets repel or push away from each other and appear to be suspended in air.

Sorting Game

Set out a magnet, two boxes and various small magnetic and non-magnetic objects such as a paper clip, a screw, a button, a piece of chalk, a piece of aluminum foil, a spoon, a kitchen magnet and a safety pin. Label one box with a picture of a magnet and the words "Things that stick." Label the other box with the words "Things that don't stick." Let the children take turns selecting an object, testing to see if it sticks to the magnet, then putting it in the appropriate box.

Magnetic Letter Games

Collect a set of upper- and lower-case plastic magnetic letters. Put the upper-case letters on one metallic surface, such as a cookie sheet, and the lower-case letters on another. Then let each child have a turn playing the letter games below.

Find the letter your first name begins with.

Pick an upper-case letter and find the matching lower-case letter.

Choose one of the letters and think of words that begin with that letter.

Say a word and find its beginning letter.

Spell your name.

Extension: Write short words on index cards and let the children spell them out with the magnetic letters.

Hint: If you do not have a set of magnetic letters, make one of your own. Cut posterboard into 2-inch squares and write a different letter of the alphabet on each one. Glue small magnets or pieces of magnetic tape to the backs of the squares.

Counting With Magnets

Give each child a magnet and a pile of paper clips. Let the children hang their paper clips, one below the other, from their magnets. Have them count how many paper clips they have hanging. Ask them why they think the paper clips hang as they do. Explain that the magnetic power is passed from paper clip to paper clip. However, it gets weaker and weaker as it is passed along.

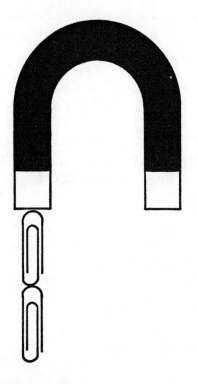

Body Magnets

Have the children pretend that their fingers, elbows, knees or toes have become magnets. Let them show you what would happen as they walk by a refrigerator or other object that has a metallic surface.

Children's Books:
• *Mickey's Magnet*, Frank Branley, (Scholastic, 1978).

Contributors:
Susan M. Paprocki, Northbrook, IL
Betty Silkunas, Lansdale, PA

MAGNIFYING GLASSES

Purchasing Magnifying Glasses

It is important to buy good magnifying glasses. The better the quality of the magnifying glass, the safer the tool and the more gained by the children. Reasonably good magnifying glasses can be purchased at drugstores or variety stores at a nominal cost.

Hint: To make these learning tools really special, put them away until the activities are introduced.

Magnifying Fingerprints

Set out an ink pad and pieces of white paper. Let the children press their fingers on the ink pad and make fingerprints on their papers. Let them use magnifying glasses to examine their own and others' fingerprints.

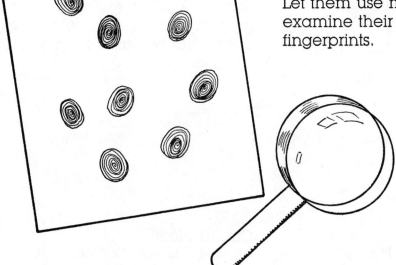

A Look at Nature

Go on a walk outdoors with the children to collect a variety of nature objects. When you get back to the room, place the objects on a table and let the children use magnifying glasses to examine them. Encourage the children to describe the colors, parts and textures of the items as seen through their magnifying glasses.

Magnified Snowflakes

If it snows in your area, do this activity during a snowfall. Take a dark cloth and a magnifying glass outside. Catch some snowflakes on the cloth. Let the children take turns using the magnifying glass to study the snowflakes. Ask them to describe the snowflakes' shapes and sizes.

Variation: Scrape a little frost from a freezer onto a dark cloth and let the children observe the ice crystals through a magnifying glass.

MAGNIFYING GLASSES

A Good Look at Food

Prepare a snack for the children. Give each child his or her snack and a magnifying glass. Let the children use the magnifying glasses to examine their snacks before eating them.

Teeny Tiny Discoveries

Give the children magnifying glasses and let them search in the room or outdoors for teeny tiny discoveries. Encourage them to look at such things as the numbers and letters on a coin, a friend's freckles, a rock, the roots of a tiny weed or the fabric of their clothes.

Preschool Detectives

Let the children use magnifying glasses to search for fingerprints in the room. Encourage them to look around the art area and examine mirrors, windows and other glass surfaces.

If You See Something Small

Sung to: "If You're Happy and You Know It"

If you see something small, magnify it.
If you see something small, magnify it.
If you see something small,
With this glass you'll see it all.
If you see something small, magnify it.

Jean Warren

Children's Books:
- *Ed Emberley's Great Thumbprint Drawing Book*, Ed Emberley, (Little Brown, 1977).
- *Snow Is Falling*, Frank Branley, (Harper, 1986).

Contributors:
Susan M. Paprocki, Northbrook, IL

Marble Art

Use a spatula to spread tempera paint in the bottom of a jelly roll pan or on a cookie sheet that has sides. Add enough marbles to cover three-fourths of the bottom of the pan. Let the children take turns placing a piece of paper on top of the marbles and rolling it around. As they do so, the marbles will roll the paint onto their papers, leaving unique designs.

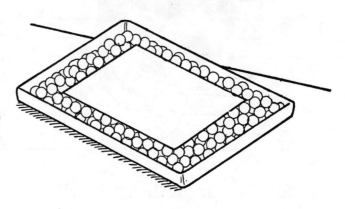

Playdough Marbles

Set out three or four bright colors of playdough. (Mix homemade playdough with powder tempera for extra bright colors.) Give each child a small jar lid. Let the children fill their lids with colorful marble shapes they roll out of the playdough.

Marble Painting

Give each child a pie tin or cake pan with a piece of construction paper cut to fit in the bottom of it. Place one or two paint-covered marbles in each child's pie tin. Let the children "paint" with their marbles by moving their pie tins all around to make their marbles roll across their papers.

Five Shiny Marbles

Line up five shiny marbles on the
floor, then recite the poem below.
Take one marble away at the end
of each verse and let the children
fill in the blank.

Five shiny marbles lying on the floor,
One shot away and that leaves _____ .

Four shiny marbles I can plainly see,
One rolled off and that leaves _____ .

Three shiny marbles, now just a few,
One left the group and that leaves _____ .

Two shiny marbles basking in the sun,
One wandered off and that leaves _____ .

One shiny marble looking for some fun,
Went off to find the others and that leaves _____ .

Susan M. Paprocki
Northbrook, IL

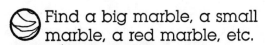

Find the Marble

Set out a tray that has different
sizes and colors of marbles on it.
Have the children stand around
the tray and ask them to:

Find a big marble, a small
marble, a red marble, etc.

Find a marble that is moving
and one that is still.

Find a marble that matches
the color of your friend's eyes,
shirt, shoes, etc.

Find two marbles that are alike
and two that are different. Tell
how they are alike and different.

Find one marble that is near
the edge of the tray and one
that is in the middle.

How Many Marbles?

Place a number of marbles in a clear plastic bag or a jar. Let the children try guessing how many marbles are in the bag. Take the marbles out and count them together. Repeat with a different number of marbles.

Counting Marbles

Put paper baking cups in a 6-cup muffin tin and number them from 1 to 6. Let the children take turns placing the corresponding number of marbles in each cup.

Hint: As the children's counting skills increase, use a 12-cup muffin tin.

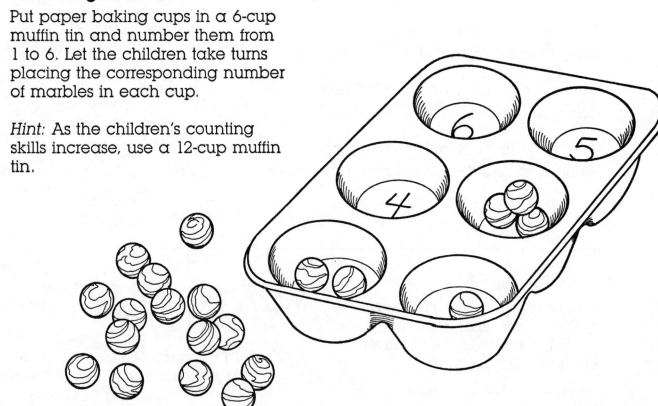

Marble Color Game

Collect or purchase solid colored marbles (available at craft and variety stores). Cut small circles out of construction paper to match the colors of the marbles and place them in a muffin tin. Set out the muffin tin and let the children sort the marbles by color into the appropriate cups.

Drop the Marble

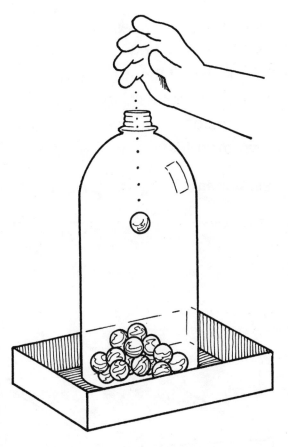

Set a plastic 2-liter bottle inside of a cardboard box. Give each child several marbles. Let the children take turns holding their marbles several inches above the neck of the bottle and trying to drop them inside. Have the children count the number of marbles that made it inside the bottle.

I Love Marbles

Sung to: ''Three Blind Mice''

Marbles red, marbles blue.
I love marbles. How about you?
I love to count them every day,
I love to shoot them when I play,
My favorite marble is big and gray.
I love marbles.

Jean Warren

Marble Shooting Game

Cut several doors in two sides of a box, as shown. Place the box on the floor. Have the children lie down a short distance from the box and try shooting marbles through the doors. Lift the box and, with the children, count the marbles that made it through the doors.

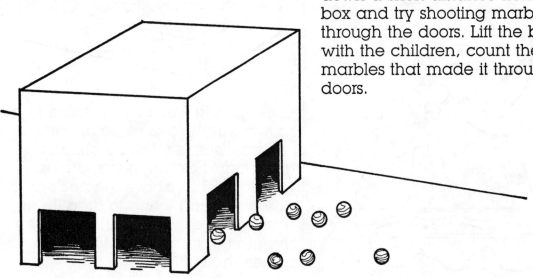

Marble Box

Invert the lid of a shoebox and tape it on top of the box along one side to make a hinged lid. Cut a 1-inch hole in the lid. Place two marbles on the lid (the edges of the lid will keep the marbles from rolling off). Have a child hold the box with two hands and tilt it back and forth until the marbles fall into the hole. Lift the lid, retrieve the marbles and let another child take a turn.

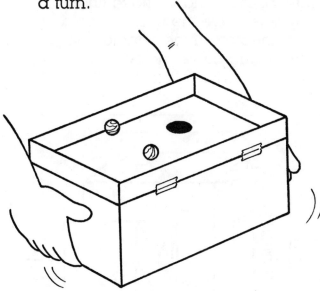

Spinning Marbles

Have the children stand in an open area. Then let them pretend to be marbles rolling and spinning around. Can they spin quickly? Can they spin slowly? What happens when they gently bump into other marbles?

Children's Books:
- *Playing Marbles*, Julie Brinckloe, (Morrow, 1988).
- *Twenty-Six Letters and Ninety-Nine Cents*, Lillian Hoban, (Greenwillow, 1987).

Contributors:
Deb Eschenbach, Ft. Wayne, IN
Susan M. Paprocki, Northbrook, IL
Melode Hurst, Grand Junction, CO

Finger Puppet Theaters

Make a finger puppet theater for each child by cutting off the bottom of a half-gallon milk carton and cutting a window in one side. Mix powder tempera paint with liquid soap to make a paint that will stick to the waxed cartons. Let the children use the paint to decorate their theaters. Allow the paint to dry. Then use non-permanent felt-tip markers to draw faces on the fingers of each child's right or left hand to make finger puppets. Have the children hold their theaters in their unmarked hands and make their finger puppets perform "on stage."

Milk Carton Wind Catchers

For each child cut a vertical "door" in each side of a milk carton. (Make sure the doors are cut so that they will all open in the same direction.) Fold the doors open and let the children paint the cartons with a powder tempera and liquid soap mixture. Punch a hole in the top of each carton and tie a piece of string through it. Hang the finished wind catchers outside and watch them twirl.

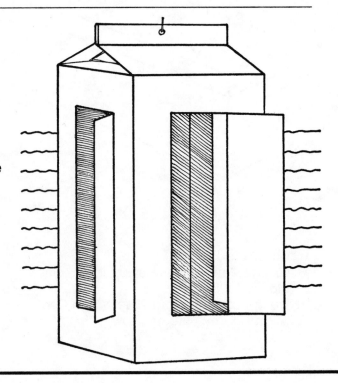

Milk Carton Bird Feeder

Cut a door in the side of a half-gallon milk carton. Fill the carton up to the level of the door with birdseed. Hang the bird feeder outside where it can be observed through a window from inside the room. Have the children keep track of the birds that visit their feeder.

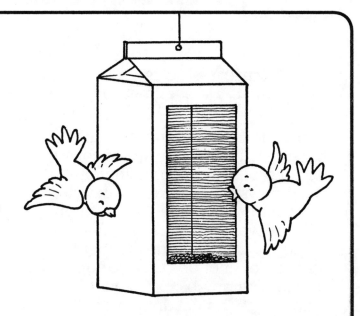

Millie Milk Carton Puppet

Thoroughly wash and dry an empty half-gallon milk carton. On the back of the carton, poke a hole through the top. Insert a piece of yarn through the hole and knot the end on the inside of the carton. Then tape the top closed and cover the entire carton with construction paper, letting the yarn hang free. Approximately one-third of the way down, cut through three sides of the carton with a craft knife, leaving the side with the yarn uncut. Use felt-tip markers to draw eyes and a nose on the top half of the carton and a mouth around the cut. Add pieces of yarn for hair.

MILK CARTONS

Milk Carton Blocks

Cut the tops off half-gallon milk cartons and discard. Rinse and dry the cartons well. To make each block, you will need two cartons. Fill one of the cartons with crumpled newspaper for extra strength, if desired. Then slide the top of one carton over the top of the other. Tape the outside edges so that the cartons cannot be pulled apart. Make as many blocks as you wish. Encourage the children to stack the blocks, count them, or just build with them.

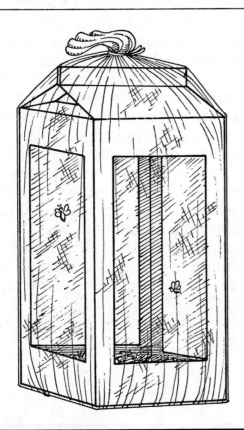

Milk Carton Bug House

Make this simple house for insects. Cut a rectangle out of each side of a clean half-gallon milk carton. Glue or tape the top closed. Help the children find one or two insects. Put the insects, along with some grass and twigs, in the milk carton. Cover the carton with an old nylon stocking and use a twist tie to fasten the nylon around the top of it. Observe the insects with the children. At the end of the day, have the children carefully return the insects to the area where they were found.

Milk Carton Banjos

For each child cut a rectangle in the side of a half-gallon milk carton. Wrap each carton with four or five large rubber bands. Give the children the milk carton banjos and let them strum their rubber band "strings." If desired, play some banjo music while the children are strumming.

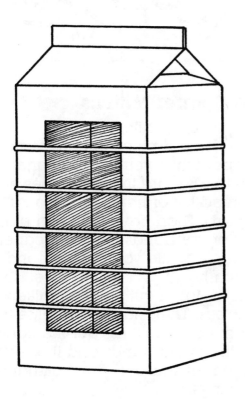

Milk Carton Snack

Give each child a glass and a half-pint carton of milk. Have the children carefully pour their milk into their glasses. Let them enjoy their milk while eating peanut butter and crackers, apple slices or any other snack foods.

Pouring Water

Fill a large dishpan with water. Set out rinsed half-pint milk cartons and plastic glasses or cups. Show the children how to hold the cartons under the water to fill them up. Then let them practice pouring the water into the plastic glasses. Have them pour the water in the glasses back into the dishpan before starting all over again.

Children's Books:
- *It Looked Like Spilt Milk*, Charles Shaw, (Harper, 1988).
- *Bugs*, Nancy Parker, (Mulberry, 1987).

Lacing Mittens

Cut large mitten shapes out of posterboard. Use a hole punch to punch holes around the edges of the shapes. Tie the end of a long piece of yarn through one of the holes in each shape. Dip the other ends of the yarn pieces in glue to stiffen them for easier lacing. Allow the glue to dry for several hours. Give the children the mitten shapes and let them lace the yarn around their mittens.

Wallpaper Mittens

Have each child place his or her hands on a piece of construction paper while you trace around them. (Be sure the child does not spread his or her fingers too far apart.) Then have the child place his or her hands on a wallpaper sample while you trace around each hand in a mitten style. Help the children cut out their mitten shapes. Then have them glue their right-hand mittens over the tracings of their right hands and their left-hand mittens over their left-hand tracings.

Color Mittens

Cut a kitten shape out of white felt. Then cut two mitten shapes out of blue felt and one mitten shape each out of red, yellow, brown, green and black felt. Place the kitten shape on a flannelboard and put a blue mitten shape on one of its paws. As you recite the poem below, place the appropriate colored mittens, one at a time, on the kitten's other paw. When the children become familiar with the poem, leave off the last word in each verse and let them supply the rhyming color word.

My poor little kitten
Lost her mitten
And started to cry, "Boo-hoo."
So I helped my kitten
To look for her mitten,
Her beautiful mitten of blue.

I found a mitten
Just right for a kitten
Under my mother's bed.
But, alas, the mitten
Was not the right mitten,
For it was colored red.

I found a mitten
Just right for a kitten
Under my father's pillow.
But, alas, the mitten
Was not the right mitten,
For it was colored yellow.

I found a mitten
Just right for a kitten
On the hand of my brother's toy clown.
But, alas, the mitten
Was not the right mitten,
For it was colored brown.

I found a mitten
Just right for a kitten
Under the laundry so clean.
But, alas, the mitten
Was not the right mitten,
For it was colored green.

I found a mitten
Just right for a kitten
Inside a grocery sack.
But, alas, the mitten
Was not the right mitten,
For it was colored black.

I found a mitten
Just right for a kitten
Inside my favorite shoe.
And this time the mitten
Was just the right mitten,
For it was colored blue!

Jean Warren

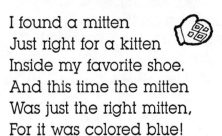

MITTENS

Mitten Weather Game

Cut pictures of snowy places and sunny places out of magazines. Then cut out construction paper mitten shapes. Ask the children to describe what the weather is like when they wear mittens. Then play this game with them. Give each of the children a mitten shape. Show them one of the magazine pictures. If it is a picture of a place where they would wear mittens, have them hold up their mitten shapes. If it is a picture of a place where they would not wear mittens, have them hide the shapes behind their backs.

Variation: Instead of using construction paper mittens, give each child a pair of real mittens. Have the children put on or take off their mittens depending on the picture you hold up.

Mitten Game

Ask the children to sit in a circle and give them each a pair of mittens. Have each child put one mitten on and place the other mitten in the middle of the circle. Mix up the pile of mittens and let the children search through it to find their mates. When they have found their matching mittens, have them put them on and sit back down in the circle.

Variation: Instead of using real mittens, cut mitten shapes out of construction paper, felt or wallpaper samples and give each child a different colored or patterned pair.

Matching Mittens

Cut pairs of mitten shapes out of different textured fabrics such as corduroy, velveteen, flannel and denim. Mix up the shapes and put them in a basket. Hang a clothesline between two chairs and clip clothespins to it. Let the children take turns finding the matching mitten shapes and hanging them on the clothesline.

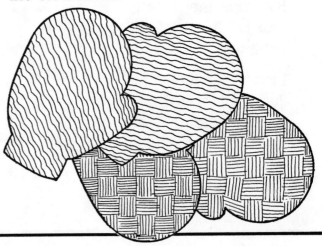

The Mitten Song

Sung to: "Twinkle, Twinkle, Little Star"

Thumbs in the thumb place,
Fingers all together!
This is the song
We sing in mitten weather.
When it is cold,
It doesn't matter whether
Mittens are wool
Or made of finest leather.
This is the song
We sing in mitten weather –
Thumbs in the thumb place,
Fingers all together!

Author Unknown

Mitten Toast

Give each of the children two pieces of mitten-shaped toast. Let them spread on peanut butter before eating their "mittens."

Variation: Cut slices of bread into mitten shapes and make mitten-shaped French toast.

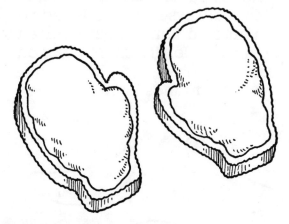

Children's Books:
- *The Mystery of the Missing Red Mitten*, Steven Kellogg, (Dial, 1977).
- *The Mitten*, Alvin Tresselt, (Scholastic, 1987).

Contributors:
Lena Goehring, Columbus, PA
Betty Silkunas, Lansdale, PA

Thumbprint Monkeys

Give each child a piece of construction paper with the outline of a tree drawn on it. Set out ink pads and felt-tip markers. Let the children make thumbprint monkeys all over their tree pictures. To create each monkey, have them press a thumb on an ink pad and make two thumbprints, one above the other, on their papers. Then let them complete their monkeys by adding faces, arms, legs and tails with felt-tip markers.

Bananas for the Monkeys

Cut five monkey shapes out of brown felt and fifteen banana shapes out of yellow felt. Number the monkeys from 1 to 5 and place them on a flannelboard. Have the children identify the number on each monkey and place that many bananas in front of it.

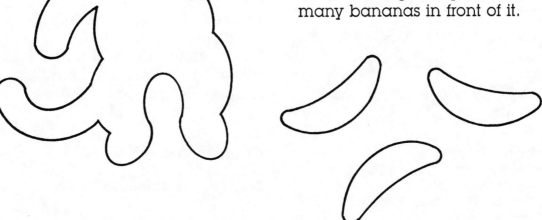

What Can a Monkey See?

Sing the song below with the children. Pause after the word "see" in the last line and point to a child to name something a monkey can see from a tree. Then finish the song. Repeat until each child has had a turn.

Sung to: "Skip to My Lou"

What can a monkey see from a tree?
What can a monkey see from a tree?
What can a monkey see from a tree?
It can see _____ from a tree.

Jean Warren

Monkey See, Monkey Do

Have the children stand in a circle. Choose one child to make a funny movement and have the other children try to imitate it. Continue until all the children have been chosen to lead funny moves.

I'm a Little Monkey
Sung to: "I'm a Little Teapot"

I'm a little monkey in the tree,
Swinging by my tail so merrily.
I can leap and fly from tree to tree,
I have lots of fun you see.

I'm a little monkey, watch me play,
Munching on bananas every day.
Lots of monkey friends to play with me,
We have fun up in the tree.

Carla C. Skjong
Tyler, MN

The Monkeys at the Zoo
Sung to: "The Farmer in the Dell"

The monkeys at the zoo,
The monkeys at the zoo.
Hi-ho, they laugh and play,
The monkeys at the zoo.

The monkeys run and hide,
The monkeys run and hide.
They like to play, then run away,
The monkeys at the zoo.

Bonnie Woodard
Shreveport, LA

Swing, Swing

Ask the children to stand in a circle and hold hands. While you recite the following poem, have them swing their arms up and down.

Little monkeys swinging in the tree,
All hold hands and swing with me.

Swing up high and swing down low,
Swing in the tree, now don't let go!

Swing, swing, like I do.
Swing like monkeys in the zoo.

Jean Warren

Children's Books:
- *Caps for Sale,* Esphyr Slobodkina, (Harper, 1947).
- *Curious George,* Margaret Rey, (Houghton Mifflin, 1941).
- *Where's Wallace?,* Hilary Knight, (Harper, 1964).

Banana Butter

Mash 3 small ripe bananas with a fork. Mix in ¾ cup peanut butter. Add ¼ teaspoon cinnamon, 1 teaspoon shredded coconut and ½ cup raisins. Blend well. Serve the banana butter on bread, crackers or fruit.

Contributors:
Sharon L. Olson, Minot, ND

NEWSPAPERS

Painting on Newspapers

Tape large sheets of newspaper to a tabletop or the floor and let the children paint on them. Then cut the papers into seasonal shapes and display them on a wall or a bulletin board. Or give the children seasonal stencils to use for creating designs on sheets of newspaper.

Variation: Hang newspaper instead of regular art paper on an easel.

Comics Collages

Set out the colored comics sections from Sunday newspapers, construction paper and glue. Have the children tear the comics into small pieces and glue them on the construction paper to create collages.

Reading the Newspaper

Look through a newspaper and mark three or four items in various sections to read to the children. (Don't cut out the items; just mark them for easy spotting.) Have the children sit in a circle. Hold the newspaper so that the children can see it and read the marked items to them.

Letter Matching

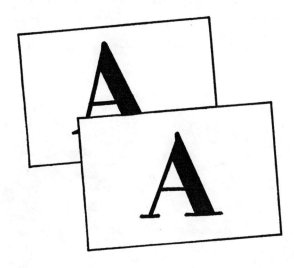

Cut matching alphabet letters out of newspaper headlines. Glue each letter to half of an index card. Mix up the cards and let the children find the matching letters.

Letter Search

Give the children sections of a newspaper and felt-tip markers. Have each child look for the letter his or her name begins with and circle it. Or have the children look for specific letters or numbers.

NEWSPAPERS

Newspaper Pictures

Cut pictures of familiar items out of newspapers. Label each picture with the item's name cut out of a headline. Let the children look at the pictures and say the names of the items.

Newspaper Props

Make these fun and inexpensive props from sheets of newspaper.

Poncho – Cut a hole in the center of a large sheet of newspaperand slip the paper over a child's head.

Sailor Hat – Fold a sheet of newspaper as illustrated below.

Twirling Skirt – Tear newspaper into strips and tape them to a piece of yarn. Tie the yarn around a child's waist.

Cone Hat – Roll a folded sheet of newspaper into a cone and secure with tape.

Can You Read the Newspaper?

Sung to: "Oh, My Darling Clementine"

Can you read
The newspaper?
Can you read it to me now?
I will watch you
Read the newspaper,
And someday I'll learn how!

Can you read
The funny pages?
Can you read them to me now?
I will watch you
Read the funny pages,
And someday I'll learn how!

Can you read
The sports pages?
Can you read them to me now?
I will watch you
Read the sports pages,
And someday I'll learn how!

Can you read
The advertisements?
Can you read them to me now?
I will watch you
Read the advertisements,
And someday I'll learn how!

Jean Warren

Children's Books:
- *Mrs. Dunphy's Dog,* Catherine O'Neill, (Viking, 1987).
- *Deadline! From News to Newspaper,* Gail Gibbon, (Harper, 1987).

Contributors:
Sarah Cooper, Arlington, TX

Nutshell Collages

Save the shells from a variety of nuts you have cracked. Break them into different sized pieces. Set out the nutshells, glue and a square of posterboard for each child. Then let the children glue the shell pieces on their squares to make collages.

Problem Solving

Show the children several different kinds of unshelled nuts. Ask them if they can think of ways to crack open the nuts to get to the meat inside. Discuss possible solutions such as pounding the shells with a rock or stepping on them. Then give each of the children several nuts and let them try out their ideas.

Pecan Pie Game

Attach five foil tart pans to squares of posterboard and number the squares from 1 to 5. Fill the tart pans with playdough to make "pies." Provide the children with a basket containing fifteen unshelled pecans. Then let them decorate the pies by placing the appropriate number of pecans on top of each one.

Nut Transfer

Set out unshelled nuts, an ice cube tray and a pair of small kitchen tongs. Let the children take turns using the tongs to place one nut in each compartment of the ice cube tray.

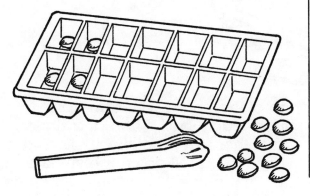

Sorting Nuts

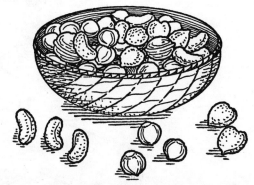

Place a variety of unshelled nuts, such as walnuts, almonds, hazelnuts and pecans, in a basket. Let the children take turns sorting the nuts by kind.

Nut Counting Game

Have the children sit in a circle and give each one six unshelled nuts. Ask a child to roll a large die and to call out the number that comes up. Then have all the children count out that many nuts. Repeat until each child has had a chance to roll the die.

Hint: Make a large die by numbering the sides of a plastic photo cube or sturdy square box with self-stick circles.

Walnut Shell Racing

For this game you will need a smooth board, several walnut shell halves and an equal number of marbles. On a table or on the floor, prop up one end of the board (or hold it up yourself) to make a slanted "race track." To play the game, let pairs of children take turns placing the shells at the top of the board with a marble under each shell. Then at a signal, have them let go of the shells and watch them roll down the track to the "finish line." You can adjust the speed of the walnut shell racers by raising or lowering the end of the board.

See the Nut Trees

Sung to: "Frere Jacques"

See the nut trees, see the nut trees,
Growing here, growing there.
Hazelnuts and walnuts,
Almonds and pecans,
Everywhere, everywhere.

Gayle Bittinger

Nutty Snacks

Serve the children a nutty snack by adding chopped nuts to your favorite recipe for pancakes, waffles, muffins, banana bread or zucchini bread.

Nut Tasting

Chop up two or three different kinds of nuts. Give each child one half of an unpeeled banana, a small amount of yogurt and a spoonful of each kind of chopped nut. Have the children gradually peel their bananas, dip them in the yogurt and then into one of the kinds of chopped nuts before taking each bite. Ask them to compare the tastes of the different nuts. Which ones do they like best?

Children's Books:
- *Frederick*, Leo Lionni, (Random House, 1967).
- *Peanut Butter and Jelly*, Nadine Westcott, (Dutton, 1988).

Contributors:
Anne Betcone, Bellevue, WA
Joyce Marshall, Whitby, Ontario
Joleen Meier, Marietta, GA

OCTOPUSES

Swimming Octopuses

Give each child a half circle cut out of white construction paper or half of a paper plate for an octopus body. Let the children use black crayons to draw on eyes. Then have them each glue eight pieces of white crepe paper to the bottom edges of their octopus bodies to make arms. Hang the finished octopuses from a string stretched across a window and watch them ''swim'' as air moves through the room.

Easy Octopus Art

For each child draw seven 5½-inch lines up from the long side of a piece of construction paper. Have the children cut along the lines on their papers to make octopus arms. When they have finished, roll each paper and tape the sides of the body together, leaving the arms free. Let the children attach self-stick circles for eyes. Then have them bend their octopus arms outward. Hang the finished products from a string or pin them on a bulletin board.

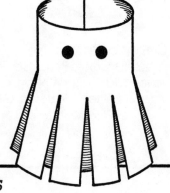

Octopus Suction Cups

An octopus has eight arms, or tentacles. On the underside of each tentacle are two rows of small round muscles that act like suction cups. Show the children pictures of an octopus and its tentacles and suckers. Talk about how the octopus uses the suckers to fasten its tentacles tightly to rocks and other objects. Then give each child a suction cup cut from an old vinyl bathmat. Let the children try sticking their suction cups to various objects in the room. What things do their cups stick to best?

Hint: The suction cups may stick better if they are moistened first.

Counting to Eight

Since an octopus has eight legs, have the children practice counting to eight in many different ways. Use the following ideas for counting or make up activities of your own.

Put away eight toys.

Pick up eight pieces of litter.

Jump up and down eight times.

Sing eight songs.

Eat eight grapes for a snack.

Make eight playdough "snakes."

Draw eight circles.

Count eight pennies.

Make eight wishes.

OCTOPUSES

Octopus Matching Game

Sometimes an octopus will change its skin color to blend in with its surroundings. Cut eight octopus shapes out of different colors of construction paper. Draw simple seascapes on eight matching colors of construction paper. Set out the seascapes and place the octopus shapes in a pile. Have the children place each octopus on its matching background.

Octopus Movements

Have four children at a time form an "octopus" by sitting on the floor with their backs facing and their arms linked. Have them open and close their legs as everyone sings the song below.

Sung to: "Little White Duck"

There are eight tentacles swimming in the ocean,
Eight tentacles making a commotion.
Who could belong to so many feet?
The octopus does, and they help it eat.
There are eight tentacles swimming in the ocean,
Swish, swish, swish.

Judy Hall
Wytheville, VA

Hot Dog Octopus

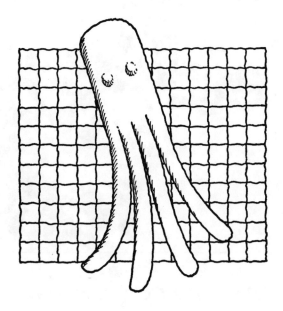

Cut slits in a hot dog two-thirds of the way up. Use a toothpick to poke two eyes near the top. Put the "Octopus hot dog" in a pan of boiling water. As it cooks, its arms will curl up and its eyes will pop out.

Popcorn Octopuses

At snacktime give each child a plate with some popcorn, softened cream cheese and shredded Mozzarella cheese on it. Have the children dip their pieces of popcorn into the cream cheese, then into the shredded cheese. The popcorn pieces will resemble tiny octopuses with shredded-cheese arms.

Octopus Partners

Give each child a crepe paper octopus made from eight 15-inch streamers knotted together. Let each child dance around the room with an octopus partner while you play music.

Children's Books:
- *Herman the Helper*, Robert Kraus, (Windmill, 1981).

Contributors:
Ellen Javernick, Loveland, CO
Susan Peters, Upland, CA
Sue Schliecker, Waukesha, WI
Betty Loew White, Amarillo, TX

ORANGES

Orange Printing

Cut several oranges in half. Let the children help you squeeze some of the juice out of the oranges. (Save the juice for snacktime, if desired.) Allow the orange halves to dry for about an hour. Place folded paper towels in shallow containers and pour on small amounts of orange tempera paint. Give the children pieces of white construction paper. Have them dip the orange halves into the paint and then press them on their papers to make prints.

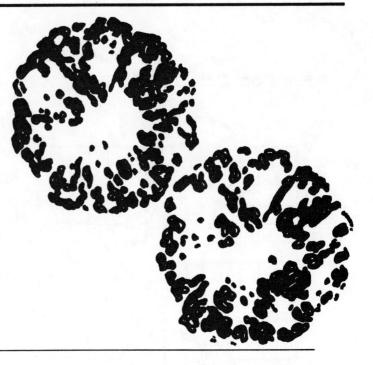

Making the Color Orange

Place three clear plastic glasses filled with water on a table. Let the children take turns dipping strips of red crepe paper into one glass and strips of yellow into another. When the water in the glasses has turned to red and yellow, let the children dip strips of both colors into the third glass and observe the new color they have created.

Sensing Oranges

Have the children sit in a circle. Pass around several oranges and have the children describe how they look and feel. Peel one of the oranges while the children listen. Give them each an orange section and ask them to tell you how the oranges smell and taste. Then sing the following song:

Sung to: "The Mulberry Bush"

What does an orange look like,
Orange look like, orange look like?
What does an orange look like?
It looks round and orange.

What does an orange feel like,
Orange feel like, orange feel like?
What does an orange feel like?
It feels a little bumpy.

What does an orange sound like,
Orange sound like, orange sound like?
What does an orange sound like?
Listen carefully.

What does an orange smell like,
Orange smell like, orange smell like?
What does an orange smell like?
It smells nice and sweet.

What does an orange taste like,
Orange taste like, orange taste like?
What does an orange taste like,
It tastes oh, so yummy!

Kathie Gonion
Elk Grove Village, IL

Picking Oranges

Cut a large tree shape out of green felt and ten orange shapes out of orange felt. Number the orange shapes from 1 to 10 with numbers or dots. Place the tree shape on a flannelboard and arrange the orange shapes on it. Let the children take turns "picking" an orange and identifying the number or counting the dots on it.

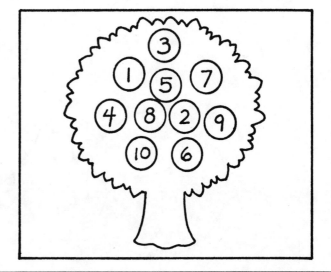

Squeeze the Oranges

Sung to: "Row, Row, Row Your Boat"

Squeeze, squeeze,
Squeeze the oranges,
Squeeze them all this way,
So we can have some orange juice
To start our sunny day.

Jean Warren

I'm a Big Juicy Orange

Sung to: "Little White Duck"

I'm a big juicy orange
Sitting in the breeze,
A big juicy orange
Waiting for a squeeze.
So if you happen to come my way,
Give me a hug and you'll make
   my day.
I'm a big juicy orange
Waiting for a squeeze.
Squeeze, squeeze, squeeze.

Jean Warren

Fresh-Squeezed Orange Juice

Set out oranges and a juicer. Cut the oranges in half. Show the children how the juicer works. Then let them take turns squeezing the orange halves with the juicer. Pour the fresh-squeezed orange juice into cups for the children to taste.

Orange Fruit Cups

Cut oranges in half. Scoop out the fruit and set the rinds aside. Cut the fruit into small pieces and put them in a bowl. Add chopped bananas, apples and grapes to the orange pieces and mix together. Fill each orange rind with a scoop of the fruit salad and serve.

Children's Books:
- *Mouse Paint*, C. Walsh, (Harcourt, 1989).
- *Eating the Alphabet*, Lois Ehlert, (Harcourt, 1989).

Contributors:
Kathy Gonion, Elk Grove Village, IL

Owl Faces

Give each child a 9-inch paper plate. Cut 7-inch squares of yellow construction paper in half diagonally to make triangles. Have the children paint the backs of their paper plates brown. When the paint has dried, help each child glue a yellow triangle on his or her plate as shown. Then have the child glue on two paper baking cups for eyes. Set out small black construction paper circles, triangles and rectangles and let the children try dropping different shapes into the "eyes" of their owls. Depending on the shapes, the owls will appear to be wide-eyed, sleepy, winking, etc. Have the children glue the shapes they like best in the bottoms of their paper baking cups.

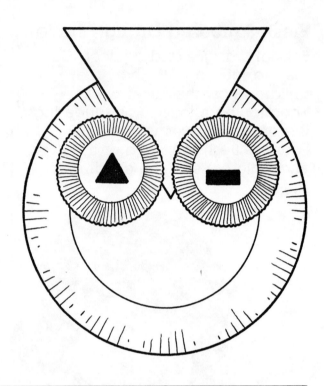

Peek-A-Boo Owl Puppets

Give each child a toilet tissue tube with a hole cut in one side about 1 inch from the bottom. Have the children color their tubes to resemble trees. Use a felt-tip marker to draw an owl face on each child's index finger. Show the children how to poke their fingers through the holes in their tubes to look like little owls peeking out of hollow trees. Let the children use their owl puppets while reciting owl poems, singing owl songs or talking to other "owls" in the room.

Wise Old Bird

Recite the following poem with the children:

A wise old owl sat in an oak.
The more he heard, the less he spoke.
The less he spoke, the more he heard.
Why aren't we all like that wise old bird?

Traditional

Facts About Owls

Share these owl facts with the children. Owls live alone and fly around at night making hooting sounds. They like to nest in dark places such as caves and hollow trees. Owls have eyes on the fronts rather than the sides of their heads. The circle of feathers around their eyes is what makes them look like "wise old birds." Owls see very well in the dark and have excellent hearing. They are the farmers' friends because they eat mice and harmful insects that destroy crops.

Whooo Is It?

For this listening game, choose one child to be the Parent Owl and have the child leave the room. Choose two or three other children to be Owlets, or baby owls. Have all the children cover their mouths with their hands, and ask only the Owlets to begin saying "Whooo, whooo." Then have the Parent Owl return to the room, listen carefully to the "whooo-ing" and try to find his or her babies. Continue the game, each time choosing different children to be the Parent Owl and the Owlets.

Owl Snacks

Cut cheese slices in half diagonally to make triangles. Give each child a piece of bologna, a cheese triangle and two round pickle slices. Let the children arrange their cheese slices on top of their bologna pieces to make owl faces. Then have them add their pickle slices for eyes.

Wise Old Owl

Sung to: "Frere Jacques"

Wise old owl, wise old owl,
In the tree, in the tree.
Who-oo are you winking at?
Who-oo are you winking at?
Is it me? Is it me?

Jean Warren

I'm a Little Gray Owl

Sung to: "I'm a Little Teapot"

I'm a little gray owl
Sitting in a tree.
A little gray owl,
There's no one but me.
I sit all night up in my tree,
The moon and the stars are all I see.

Jean Warren

Children's Books:
- *Owl Moon*, Jane Yolen, (Putnam, 1987).
- *Owl and the Pussycat*, Edward Lear, (Holiday, 1982).
- *Owl Lake*, Keizaburo Tejima, (Putnam, 1987).

Contributors:
Ellen Javernick, Loveland, CO

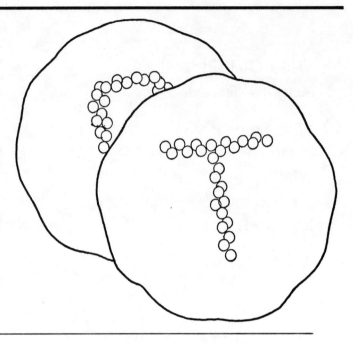

Blueberry Pancake Art

Cut large pancake shapes out of brown construction paper. Use a hole punch to punch "blueberry" circles out of blue construction paper. Give each child a pancake shape with the beginning letter of his or her first name written on it. Have the children trace over their letters with cotton swabs dipped in glue. Then have them sprinkle the blueberry circles on top of the glue and shake off the excess.

Pancake Man Puppets

Cut 3-inch circles out of brown posterboard. Cut two finger holes in the bottom of each circle as shown to make a Pancake Man puppet. Give each child a puppet. Let the children decorate their puppets with crayons or felt-tip markers. Have the children each put two fingers through the holes in their puppets to make them walk or run. Let them use their puppets while they sing the song on page 170.

Pancake Games

Cut 3-inch "pancakes" out of corrugated cardboard and let the children use them to play the following games:

Hold a pie pan containing a pancake with both hands. Toss up the pancake and try catching it in the pan.

Walk across the room and back while balancing a pancake on a pancake turner.

Stand beside a large frying pan placed on the floor and drop in a designated number of pancakes.

Use a pancake turner to turn over pancakes that have been previously marked with colors or numbers to find matching pairs.

Stack pancakes on paper plates and count the number of pancakes in each stack.

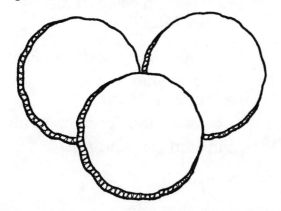

Blueberry Pancake Game

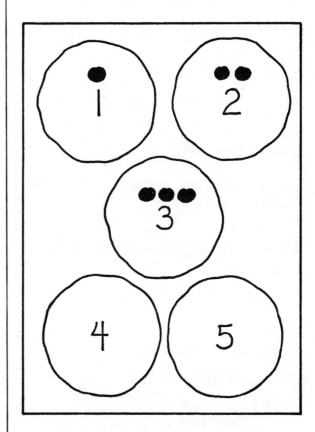

Cut five pancake shapes out of brown felt and fifteen blueberry shapes out of blue felt. Use a felt-tip marker to number the pancakes from 1 to 5. Place the pancakes on a flannelboard. Ask the children to identify the number on each pancake and place the corresponding number of blueberries on it.

PANCAKES

Have You Seen the Pancake Man?
Sung to: "The Muffin Man"

Have you seen the Pancake Man,
The Pancake Man, the Pancake
    Man?
Have you seen the Pancake Man
Who jumped from the skillet
    and ran and ran?

He jumped from the skillet down to
    the floor,
To the floor, to the floor.
He jumped from the skillet down to
    the floor
And ran right out the door.

He called to the wife as he ran,
As he ran, as he ran.
He called to the wife as he ran,
"You can't catch me, I'm the
    Pancake Man!"

He called to the daughter
    as he ran,
As he ran, as he ran.
He called to the daughter
    as he ran,
"You can't catch me, I'm the
    Pancake Man!"

He called to the farmer as he ran,
As he ran, as he ran.
He called to the farmer as he ran,
"You can't catch me, I'm the
    Pancake Man!"

He called to the cow as he ran,
As he ran, as he ran.
He called to the cow as he ran,
"You can't catch me, I'm the
    Pancake Man!"

He called to the dog as he ran,
As he ran, as he ran.
He called to the dog as he ran,
"You can't catch me, I'm the
    Pancake Man!"

He called to the cat as he ran,
As he ran, as he ran.
He called to the cat as he ran,
"You can't catch me, I'm the
    Pancake Man!"

Have you seen the Pancake Man,
The Pancake Man,
    the Pancake Man?
Have you seen the Pancake Man
Who ran and ran and ran?

Jean Warren

Blueberry Pancakes

Beat 1 egg in a bowl. Add 1 cup buttermilk, 2 tablespoons vegetable oil, 1 cup flour, 1 tablespoon sugar, 1 teaspoon baking powder, ½ teaspoon soda and ½ teaspoon salt. Mix well. Add ½ cup fresh blueberries (or use frozen blueberries, thawed and drained). Pour the batter in spoonfuls on a hot griddle. Cook until golden brown, turning once. Makes 10 pancakes.

Dutch Pancakes

Heat an empty 8- or 9-inch pie pan in the oven. Melt 1 tablespoon butter or margarine in the bottom of the pan. Process 2 eggs, ½ cup flour and ½ cup milk in a blender. Pour the mixture into the hot pie pan. Bake 25 minutes at 425 degrees. Fill the baked pie shell with ½ cup plain yogurt and top with 1 cup mashed berries. (Raspberries or strawberries are delicious.) If desired, mash the berries with 2 tablespoons unsweetened frozen apple juice concentrate. Makes 6 servings.

Children's Books:
- *Cloudy With a Chance of Meatballs*, Judi Barrett, (Macmillan, 1978).
- *Pancakes for Breakfast*, Tomie DePaola, (Harcourt, 1978).
- *Runaway Pancake*, Joan Tate, (Larousse, 1980).

PAPER BAGS

Paper Bag Art

Give each child a square or a rectangle cut from a large paper bag. Set out various colors of tempera paint and paint brushes. Let the children paint designs on their squares. Have them carefully crumple up their papers, then uncrumple them and lay them out flat. Ask the children to describe what happened to their painted designs. When the paint has dried, use a cool iron to remove the wrinkles from the papers.

Snow Pals

Set out white paper lunch bags and newspaper. Let the children fill the bags with pieces of crumpled newspaper. Staple the top of each bag closed and tie a piece of string tightly around the middle of the bag to make a snow pal. Let the children decorate their snow pals with felt-tip markers or by gluing on buttons and construction paper hat shapes.

Paper Bag Hats

For each child cut several inches off the top of a paper bag. Roll down the tops of the bags to make hats with brims. Let the children decorate their paper bag hats with felt-tip markers or crayons. Or have them glue on collage materials such as buttons, glitter, feathers, fabric scraps and pieces of yarn.

Mystery Bags

Give each child a paper bag. Have the children take their bags home with instructions to bring them back the next day with a favorite toy inside. Have the children sit in a circle with their mystery bags. Let each child give clues about the object in his or her bag while the other children try to guess what it is.

Counting Bags

Number five small paper bags from 1 to 5. Fold down the top of each bag so that it will stay open. Set out the bags and fifteen counters, such as buttons or game chips. Let the children take turns identifying the numbers on the bags and putting in the corresponding numbers of counters.

Paper Bag Book

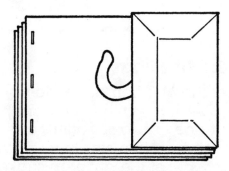 

Cut 2 inches off the tops of several paper lunch bags. Place the bags on top of one another with the flaps on the right. Then staple the bags together on the left-hand side to make a book. Use felt-tip markers to draw a picture under each flap so that part of the picture is visible when the flap is closed. If desired, select a theme for the book, such as animals, holidays or circus characters. As the children look through the book, have them try to guess what is hidden beneath each flap before lifting the flap up.

Variation: Instead of drawing a picture, glue a picture cut out of a magazine under each flap.

Brown Bag

Have the children sit in a circle. Set a large brown paper bag in the middle. Ask the children, one at a time, to find something brown to put in the bag. While each child is searching, have the rest of the children sing the following song:

Sung to: "Pop! Goes the Weasel"

It's your turn to find something brown,
Now, we don't want to nag.
Just pick it up and bring it right here,
And put it in the bag.

Gayle Bittinger

Shaking Bags

Fill pairs of small paper bags with different things such as paper clips, bells, dried beans and feathers. Fold down the tops of the bags and staple them closed. Let the children shake the bags and try to find those that make the same sounds.

Rhythm Bags

Let the children decorate small paper bags with felt-tip markers. Put one or two spoonfuls of rice in each bag and staple the tops closed. Let the children shake their rhythm bags and parade around the room while you play marching music.

Paper Bag Toss

Fold down the top of a large brown paper bag. Place the bag on the floor. Have the children stand away from the bag, crumple up pieces of newspaper and try tossing them into the bag. Let the children stand closer to or farther away from the bag depending on their ages and abilities.

Paper Bag Snacks

Pack finger foods such as carrot and celery sticks, crackers and cheese or banana chunks in paper bags. Let the children take their paper bag snacks outside to eat. Or let them have an indoor picnic and eat their snacks on a blanket spread out on the floor.

Popcorn Bag Snack

Let the children help you pop a big batch of popcorn. Give them each a small paper bag and add a scoop of popcorn. Set out small bowls of various popcorn toppings such as melted butter, grated Cheddar cheese, Parmesan cheese and taco seasoning. Let the children each choose one or two of the popcorn toppings for you to add to their bags. Then have them close their bags, shake the popcorn and toppings together and enjoy their treat.

Children's Books:
- *Playbook*, Gwenda Turner, (Viking, 1986).
- *The Paper Bag Princess*, Robert Munsch, (Firefly, 1980).

Paper Cup Printing

Make paint pads by placing folded paper towels in shallow containers and adding a small amount of tempera paint to each one. Set out a variety of sizes of paper cups. Have the children press the rims or ends of the cups on the paint pads, then onto pieces of construction paper. Let them cover their papers with circle designs or have them try making circle creatures.

Pop-Up Puppet

Give each child a Styrofoam ball with a straw stuck in it and a paper cup. (Make sure the Styrofoam ball is small enough to fit inside the cup.) Let the children turn their Styrofoam balls into faces by adding felt-tip features and gluing on yarn hair. Help each child poke a hole in the bottom of his or her cup. Then have the children stick their straws down into their cups and out the holes in the bottoms. Show the children how to make their puppets pop up and down.

Cup Windsocks

Give each child a paper cup with the bottom cut off. Set out brushes and tempera paint and let the children paint their cups. Allow the paint to dry. Cut various colors of tissue paper into 1- by 6-inch strips. Have the children glue the tissue paper strips around the wide ends of their cups. Attach a piece of string to the narrow end of each child's cup to complete.

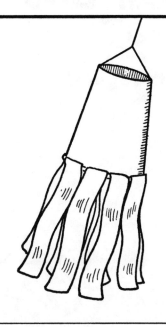

Paper Cup People

Have each child use felt-tip markers to draw a face on the side of a plain paper cup. Let the children fill their cups with dirt, then sprinkle grass seeds on top. Have them add water as necessary to keep the dirt moist. Soon their paper cup people will be growing grass "hair."

PAPER CUPS

Weighing With Paper Cups

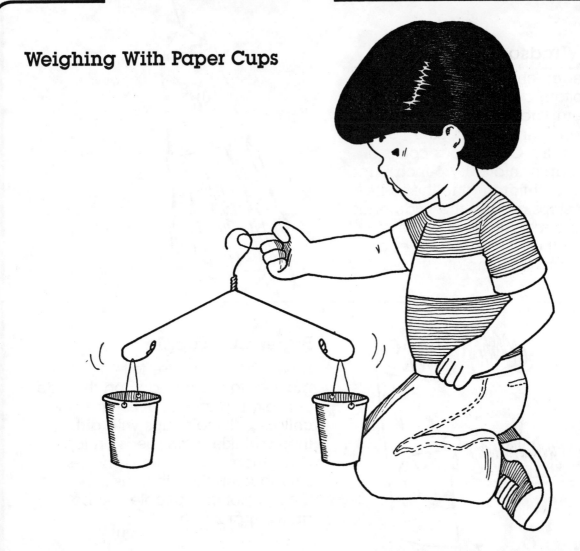

Cut the middle section out of the bottom of a wire coat hanger and cover the sharp ends with masking tape. Punch two holes in the rims of each of two paper cups. Attach a 6-inch piece of string to the holes in each of the cups. Hang the cups from the cut ends of the coat hanger and bend up the ends of the hanger to keep the cups from falling off. Have the children sit in a circle. Select two small items such as a penny and a crayon. Ask the children which one they think is the heaviest. Then put the penny in one of the cups and the crayon in the other. Hold the balance up and ask the children which is heaviest. Repeat with other items.

Phone Time

Use paper cups to make a pretend phone. Fasten the side of one paper cup to one end of a toilet tissue tube and the side of another cup to the other end. Tie a piece of yarn to the bottom of one of the paper cups. Attach the other end of the yarn to a small box. Use a felt-tip marker to draw a rotary dial or push buttons on the top of the box. Make two or three phones and let the children use them to call up and talk with one another.

Paper Cup Hiding Game

Set out three paper cups in a row and have a child place a bean under one of the cups. While the children watch, move the cups around. Ask the children to guess which cup the bean is under. Let one of the children who guessed correctly hide the bean next.

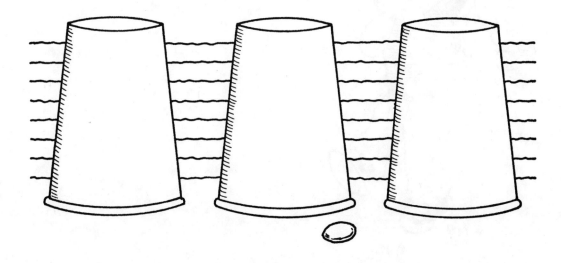

Stacking Paper Cups

Give each child three or four different sized paper cups. Have the children decorate their cups with felt-tip markers. Then let them have fun stacking their cups, one inside the other, and lining them up from smallest to largest.

Humming Cups

Cut the bottoms off paper cups. Place a piece of waxed paper across the top of each cup and secure it with a rubber band. Have each child take one of the cups and blow on the waxed paper to make a humming sound. Let the children march around the room while they play their humming cups.

Watermelon Popsicles

Blend 1 cup seedless watermelon chunks, 1 cup orange juice and 1 cup water together in a blender. Pour into small paper cups and place in a freezer. When partially frozen, insert Popsicle sticks or small plastic spoons for handles. Continue freezing. Pour hot water over the bottoms of the cups to remove the Popsicles.

Snack Cups

Serve each child three or four paper cups filled with different snack foods such as popcorn, juice, grapes and cheese cubes.

Children's Books:
- *The Paper Party,* Don Freeman, (Viking, 1974).
- *Picnic,* Emily McCully, (Harper, 1984).

Contributors:
Sophia Drake, Jamaica, NY

Dyeing Pasta

Put 2 tablespoons water and 10 drops food coloring in a recloseable plastic bag. Add 1 cup uncooked pasta, seal the bag and shake until the desired color is reached. Pour out the excess water and put the pasta on paper towels to dry.

Pasta Collages

Set out a variety of shapes and sizes of pasta. Give the children pieces of brightly colored posterboard cut into macaroni shapes. Let them glue the pasta all over their shapes to create collages.

Variation: Dye pasta shapes and let the children glue them to pieces of white posterboard cut into macaroni shapes.

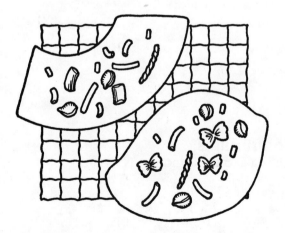

Pasta Necklaces

Dye shapes of "stringable" pasta, such as salad macaroni, wheels and rigatoni, in several different colors. Dip the ends of 2-foot pieces of yarn in glue (to make the yarn easier to string). Allow the glue to dry. Give each child one of the yarn pieces. Let the children string the colored pasta on their yarn. If desired, encourage them to make patterns with the pasta shapes and colors. Then tie the ends of each child's yarn piece together to make a necklace.

Variation: Let the children paint rigatoni noodles with tempera paints. Allow the noodles to dry. Then let the children use them to make pasta necklaces.

Cooking Pasta

Boil a pot of water and add spaghetti noodles. While the spaghetti is cooking, show the children some uncooked noodles. Ask them what they think the spaghetti will look like when it is done. Take the cooked noodles out of the pot and run them under cold water before showing them to the children. How are the cooked and the uncooked noodles different? How are they the same?

Pasta Sorting

Set out a muffin tin and a variety of small pasta shapes such as macaroni, bow ties, spirals and wheels. Let the children take turns sorting the pasta pieces by shape into the muffin tin.

Variation: Dye one kind of pasta shape six different colors and let the children sort the pieces by color.

Pasta Counting

Use a felt-tip marker to number ten paper bowls from 1 to 10. Set out the bowls along with another bowl filled with pasta shapes such as shells or spirals. Let the children take turns selecting one of the bowls, identifying the number on it and putting in that number of pasta shapes.

Pasta Matching

Select pairs of different pasta shapes. Glue each piece of pasta to an index card. Mix up the cards and let the children find the matching pairs.

Variation: Use just one kind of pasta and glue matching numbers of pieces to the cards.

Moving Like Pasta

Play music and encourage the children to move around the room like different types of pasta. Offer suggestions such as "Move like a tall stiff spaghetti noodle; Move like a wet limp spaghetti noodle; Move like a pasta wheel; Pretend that you are a piece of rigatoni and move like a log; Move like a wavy lasagna noodle."

Pasta Shapes Song

Sung to: ''Up on the Housetop''

I love pasta, yes I do,
Noodles and twists are but a few.
Then there's spaghetti and bow ties,
Wheels and macaroni any size.
I love pasta, yum, yum, yum.
I love pasta in my tum.
Pasta is so fun to eat,
Pasta is a special treat.

Gayle Bittinger

Pasta Snack

Cook several different kinds of pasta shapes according to their package directions. Make spaghetti sauce or heat up sauce from a jar. Let each child put a small amount of the pasta shapes he or she chooses into a bowl and top it off with a spoonful of spaghetti sauce.

Children's Books:
- *Strega Nona*, Tomie DePaola, (Prentice Hall, 1975).
- *More Spaghetti I Say*, Rita Gelman, (Scholastic, 1987).

Contributors:
Fawn D. Bostick, Allentown, PA

Muddy Pigs

Cut large pig shapes out of pink butcher paper. Give each child a pig shape with a small amount of brown fingerpaint in the center of it. Let the children cover their pig shapes with the brown fingerpaint "mud."

Pig Faces

Cut pig face shapes out of pink construction paper. Give each child a face shape, two small black construction paper circles and a large black button. Let the children glue on their small circles for eyes and their buttons for noses. Have them add other features with felt-tip markers, if desired.

Variation: Instead of using buttons, cut circles out of black construction paper and use a hole punch to punch two holes in each one.

Pig Facts

Despite their reputation for being dirty, pigs are actually the cleanest of all the animals on the farm. When pigs roll in the mud, it is to keep themselves cool and to prevent their skin from getting sunburned. Pigs are also quite smart and can be taught to do tricks. A mother pig is called a "sow," and a father pig is called a "boar."

Pig Noses

Cut 2-inch circles out of pink construction paper. Use a black felt-tip marker to color two small circles in the center of each one. Attach a circle to each child's nose with a loop of tape rolled sticky side out. Let the children pretend to be pigs and oink and roll around the room. Have them also wear their noses while they sing songs about pigs.

Counting Pigs

Cut ten pig shapes out of pink felt and a big mud puddle shape out of brown felt. Place the puddle shape on a flannelboard. As you sing the first verse of the following song, place the pig shapes on the mud puddle, one at a time. Then remove the pigs as you sing the last verse.

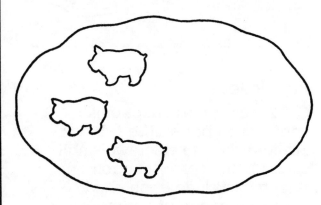

Sung to: "Ten Little Indians"

One little, two little, three little pigs,
Four little, five little, six little pigs,
Seven little, eight little, nine little pigs.
Ten are in the mud.

All are pink with pudgy noses,
They don't smell a bit like roses,
Curly tails that look like hoses.
Rolling in the mud.

Ten little, nine little, eight little pigs,
Seven little, six little, five little pigs,
Four little, three little, two little pigs.
One is in the mud.

Judy Hall
Wytheville, PA

Out in the Barnyard

Sung to: "Down by the Station"

Out in the barnyard,
Early in the morning,
You can hear the piglets
Squealing up a storm.
Here comes the momma pig,
She will feed her babies,
Oink, oink, oink, oink, on the farm.

Judy Hall
Wytheville, PA

The Pigs Are Pink and Plump

Sung to: "The Farmer in the Dell"

The pigs are pink and plump,
The pigs are pink and plump.
They keep cool in mud all day,
The pigs are pink and plump.

The pigs have curly tails,
The pigs have curly tails.
The mother pig is called a sow,
The pigs have curly tails.

The piglets are so cute,
The piglets are so cute.
The piglets are the baby pigs,
The piglets are so cute.

Carla C. Skjong
Tyler, MN

Children's Books:
- *Pigs, Pigs, Pigs,* Robert Munsch, (Firefly, 1989).
- *Pig's Wedding,* Helme Heine, (Macmillan, 1986).
- *Perfect the Pig,* Susan Jeschke, (Scholastic, 1985).

Pink Pig-Sicles

Mix together 2 cups plain yogurt, one 12-ounce can unsweetened frozen apple-cranberry juice concentrate and 2 teaspoons vanilla. Pour the mixture into small paper cups and insert plastic spoons for handles. Chill in the freezer until set, then serve as treats for snacktime. Makes 8 to 10 servings.

Pine Cone Collages

Pull the scales off of pine cones. Give the children pieces of poster-board cut into pine cone shapes. Let the children use paintbrushes to spread glue over their shapes. Then have them arrange the pine cone scales on the glue.

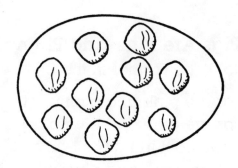

Pine Cone Art

Let the children help you pull the scales off of pine cones. Have them use the scales for the following art projects:

Flowers – Paint the scales red, pink, yellow and orange. Arrange and glue the scales in flower shapes on construction paper.

Roofs – Draw house shapes on construction paper and glue the scales to the roof areas.

Trees – Glue the scales in tree trunk shapes on construction paper. Add branches and leaves with felt-tip markers.

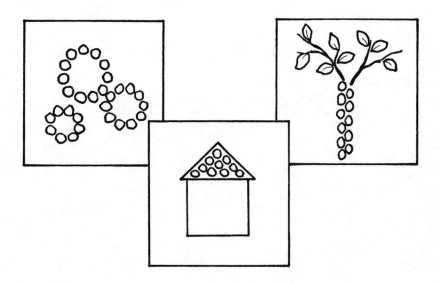

Pine Cone Turkeys

Set out pine cones and playdough Have each child put a small amount of the playdough on the side of a pine cone and place the pine cone on a table, playdough side down. (The playdough keeps the pine cones from rolling.) Let the children glue colored construction paper feather shapes between the scales at the fat ends of their pine cones. Then give them turkey head shapes cut out of construction paper. Have them glue the shapes at the narrow ends of their cones to complete their turkeys.

Counting Pine Cones

Set out a box of pine cones. Ask the children to count out three pine cones, five pine cones, etc. Then have them each select a pine cone and pull the scales off of it. Ask them to count the scales. Have them compare numbers. Which pine cone had the most scales? Which had the least?

Pine Cone Carry

Place a spoon and a basket filled with pine cones at one end of the room and an empty basket at the other end. Let the children take turns balancing a pine cone on the spoon, walking carefully across the room and putting the cone in the other basket.

Pine Cone Flannelboard Game

Cut five evergreen tree shapes out of green felt and five pine cone shapes out of brown felt. Number the tree shapes from 1 to 5. Number the pine cone shapes with dots from 1 to 5. Place the tree shapes on a flannelboard. Have the children take turns selecting a pine cone, counting the dots on it and placing it on the appropriate tree.

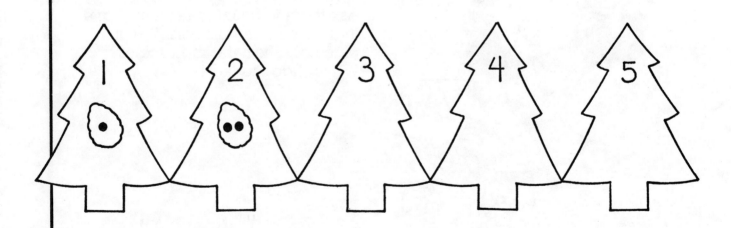

Pick Up the Pine Cones

Sung to: "The Paw Paw Patch"

Pick up the pine cones, put 'em in the basket,
Pick up the pine cones, put 'em in the basket,
Pick up the pine cones, put 'em in the basket,
Down in the forest oh, so green.

Jean Warren

Pine Cone Carrot Balls

Cream together a 3-ounce package of softened cream cheese, ½ cup finely shredded Cheddar cheese, and 1 tablespoon unsweetened frozen apple juice concentrate. Stir in 1 cup finely grated carrots. Then form the mixture into balls and roll them in ½ cup finely chopped walnuts.

Children's Books:
- *Annie and the Wild Animals*, Jan Brett, (Houghton Mifflin, 1985).
- *Deep in the Forest*, Brinton Turkle, (Dutton, 1987).

Contributors:
Ellen Javernick, Loveland, CO

PLAYING CARDS

Queen of Hearts Mural

Separate the heart suit from an old deck of playing cards. Cut sheets of a 3- by 3-inch Post-it brand note pad into fourths so that part of the sticky strip is on each piece. Then cut small hearts out of construction paper. Hang a long piece of butcher paper on a wall at the children's eye level. Cut more hearts out of construction paper to make a simple ''Queen of Hearts'' as shown above. Attach the Queen of Hearts to the butcher paper.

Then give each child four pieces of the Post-it brand note pad strips, a heart playing card and a small paper heart. Let the children arrange the strips on their cards like arms and legs. To complete their heart people, have them glue their paper hearts to the tops of their cards for heads and add faces with felt-tip markers. Finally, attach the heart people to the butcher paper in rows next to the Queen of Hearts.

Playing Card Necklaces

Punch holes in the tops of old playing cards. Give each child several cards and a piece of yarn with one end knotted and the other end taped to make a ''needle.'' Have the children string their cards on their yarn. Tie the ends of each yarn piece together and let the children wear their playing card necklaces around their necks.

Deal-A-Story

Have the children sit in a circle. Deal two or three playing cards face down to each child. Choose one child to turn over a card. Use the number or picture on the card as you begin telling a story. Then continue around the circle, letting each child turn over a card, and incorporate the numbers and pictures into your story. A sample story would be as follows:

(Child turns over a ten.)
Ten little rabbits went to town.

(Next child turns over a four.)
They went to four houses
    looking for food.

(Next card is a queen.)
At the last house they met a
    beautiful lady.

(Next card is a seven.)
She gave them seven carrots.

(Next card is a jack.)
As the rabbits started to leave,
    a little boy chased them.

(Next card is a two.)
They ran down two paths that led
    into the woods.

(Next card is a three.)
In the woods they found three
    holes which they jumped into
    safely with all their carrots.

Continue playing until each child has turned over at least one card.

Hint: Let older children take turns being the storyteller.

Playing Card Puzzles

Cut several playing cards into three or four pieces each. Place the pieces of each card in a separate pile and let the children take turns putting the mini puzzles together. For a more challenging game, mix the pieces of two or three cards together and let the children sort them out before putting the puzzles together.

PLAYING CARDS

Playing Card Toss

Make a line on the floor with a piece of masking tape. Place a basket or a box a reasonable distance away from the tape. Have the children take turns standing behind the line and tossing playing cards into the container.

Playing Card Number Game

Place all the number cards from an old deck of playing cards in a pile. Let the children take turns drawing a card from the pile and naming the number or counting the shapes on it. Let the children keep the cards they draw, if desired.

Matching Playing Cards

Take out several matching pairs from two decks of playing cards. Mix up the pairs. Let the children take turns finding the matching cards.

Playing Card Patterns Game

Collect two or three decks of playing cards with different patterns on the backs. Mix up all the cards and let the children sort them by pattern.

Sorting Playing Cards

Set out the ace, two, three and four cards from each suit in a deck of playing cards. Let the children sort the cards by numbers (1, 2, 3 and 4), suits (hearts, clubs, spades and diamonds) or colors (red and black).

Playing Card Shapes Games

Mark each of four boxes with one of these shapes: a heart, a club, a spade and a diamond. Select four or five cards of each suit from a deck of playing cards. Give a child the boxes and the cards. Let the child pick up the cards, identify the shapes on them and place them in the appropriate boxes.

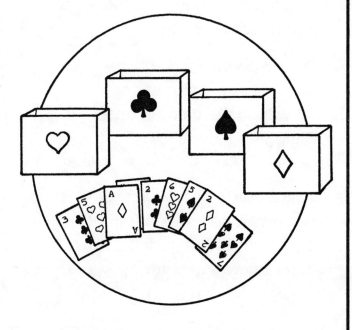

PLAYING CARDS

Everybody Take a Card

Separate the ace, two, three and four cards from a deck of playing cards and hold them in your hand. While you sing the first verse of the song below, have each child take one of the cards and sit down in a circle. Together, sing and act out the rest of the song.

Sung to: "Mary Had a Little Lamb"

Everybody take a card,
Take a card, take a card.
Everybody take a card,
Then we'll play a game.

If your card has the number one,
The number one, the number one.
If your card has the number one,
Hop aboard my train.

Off will go the cards of one,
Cards of one, cards of one.
Off will go the cards of one,
Chugging round the room.
  (Chug around room, then sit down.)

If your card has the number two,
The number two, the number two.
If your card has the number two,
Hop aboard my plane.

Off will go the cards of two,
Cards of two, cards of two.
Off will go the cards of two,
Flying round the room.
  (Fly around room, then sit down.)

If your card has the number three,
The number three, the number
    three.
If your card has the number three,
Hop aboard my car.

Off will go the cards of three,
Cards of three, cards of three.
Off will go the cards of three,
Driving round the room.
  (Drive around room, then sit down.)

If your card has the number four,
The number four, the number four.
If your card has the number four,
Hop aboard my boat.

Off will go the cards of four,
Cards of four, cards of four.
Off will go the cards of four,
Sailing round the room.
  (Sail around room, then sit down.)

Jean Warren

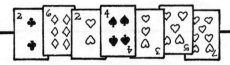

Playing Card Exercises

Separate the number cards from a deck of playing cards and hold them in your hand. Have the children stand in a circle around you. Ask a child to draw a card and identify the number on it. Then name an exercise and have all the children do it that number of times. For example, if the card drawn was a six, have the children jump up and down or touch their toes six times. Continue until each child has had a chance to draw a card.

Variation: Let the child who draws the card name the exercise as well.

Playing Card Snacks

Use cookie cutters to cut cheese slices into heart, club, spade and diamond shapes. Place the cheese shapes on crackers and serve.

Children's Books:
- *The Missing Tarts,* B.G. Hennessy, (Viking, 1989).
- *King Bidgood's in the Bathtub,* Audrey Wood, (Harcourt, 1986).

Treasure Pockets

Fold large paper plates in half. Use a hole punch to punch holes along the folds and halfway up the sides of the plates, leaving the tops open. On each plate tie one end of a piece of yarn through one of the holes. Tape the other end of the yarn piece to make a "needle." Have the children lace the yarn around the plates to make pockets. Then let them decorate their pockets with stickers. Write each child's name and the words "Treasure Pocket" on his or her plate.

TIM'S TREASURE POCKET

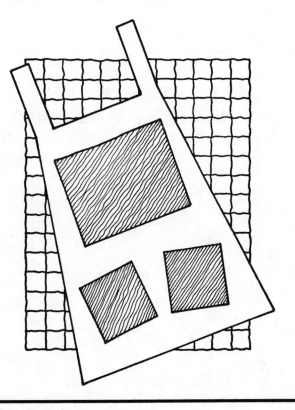

Apron Pockets

Cut apron shapes out of butcher paper and pocket shapes out of fabric. Give the children each an apron shape. Let them glue the pocket shapes on their aprons any way they wish.

In My Pockets

Wear an apron or other item of clothing that has five pockets. Put the following five objects in the pockets: a toy frog, a toy car, a rubber ball, a toy bunny and a toy dog. Then recite the poem below and take out each object as it is mentioned.

The things in my pockets are lots
   of fun,
I will show you one by one.

In my first pocket is a frog,
I found him sitting on a log.

In my second pocket is a car,
It can race off very far.

In my third pocket is a ball,
I can bounce it on a wall.

In my fourth pocket is a bunny,
She twitches her nose and looks
   so funny.

In my fifth pocket is a dog,
He's a friend of my little frog.

In my pockets my things hide,
Do you have pockets with
   things inside?

Sue Schliecker
Waukesha, WI

Feelie Pocket

Wear an apron that has at least one pocket. Put a familar object in the pocket. Ask a child to come up and feel the object in your pocket and try to guess what it is while you recite the poem below. Then have the child tell what he or she thinks the object is.

Something's in my apron pocket,
Oh my, what can it be?
Can you let your fingers guess,
Without a peek to see?

Teaching Pockets

Cut four to six large pocket shapes out of different colors of felt and sew them on a butcher-style apron. Then use the apron to play the following learning games.

Color Pockets – Discuss the apron pocket colors and ask the children to find small matching colored objects around the room. Have them put the objects in the appropriate pockets.

Beginning Sounds Pockets – Cut different alphabet letters out of felt and place them on the pockets. Provide a collection of small objects whose names begin with those letters and ask the children to put them in the appropriate pockets.

Number Pockets – Cut different numerals out of felt and place them on the pockets. Ask the children to put corresponding numbers of small objects in the pockets.

Alphabet Pockets – Cut different upper-case letters out of felt and place them on the pockets. Write cooresponding lower-case letters on posterboard squares and ask the children to put them in the appropriate pockets.

Shape Pockets – Cut different basic shapes (a circle, a square, a triangle, a star, etc.) out of felt and place them on the pockets. Cut matching shapes out of posterboard and ask the children to put them in the appropriate pockets.

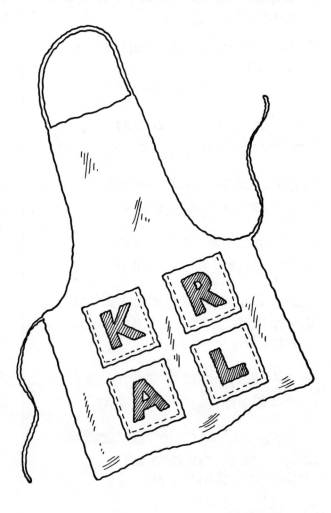

Mary Has a Pocket

Have the children sit in a circle. Talk about all the clothes they wear that have pockets. Then sing the song below, substituting one of the children's names for "Mary" and the name of the article of clothing he or she is wearing that has pockets for "dress." If the child has no pockets on his or her clothes, sing the alternate verse.

Sung to: "Mary Wore a Red Dress"

Mary has a pocket,

A pocket, a pocket.

Mary has a pocket

On her dress today.

Alternate verse: "Mary has no pockets on her dress today."

Adapted Traditional

Children's Books:
* *Katy No-Pocket*, Emmy Payne, (Houghton Mifflin, 1944).
* *Pocket for Corduroy*, Don Freeman, (Viking, 1978).

Pocket Sandwiches

Use pita bread to make pocket sandwiches. Prepare a favorite sloppy joe recipe. Cut rounds of pita bread in half and open them up to look like pockets. Put a scoop of the sloppy joe mixture in each pita half and top with grated cheese.

Variation: Spread peanut butter inside pita bread halves and add raisins, bananas, carrots or sunflower seeds.

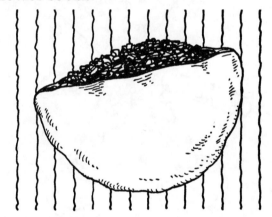

Contributors:
Sue Schliecker, Waukesha, WI

Pretzel Sculptures

Set out stick pretzels and play-dough. Have the children roll the playdough into balls. Then let them use the playdough balls and the pretzels to create sculptures by sticking the ends of the pretzels into the playdough.

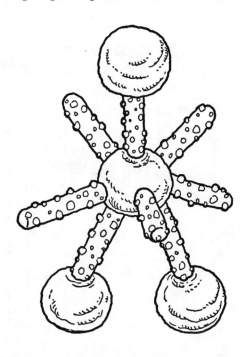

Variation: Let the children create edible sculptures by using peanut butter playdough. To make the dough, mix together equal amounts of peanut butter and nonfat dry milk. Add honey to taste, if desired.

See the Pretzels

Cut ten stick pretzel shapes out of brown felt and place a number of them on a flannelboard. Sing the song below and count the pretzels at the end. Repeat the song, plac-ing a different number of pretzels on the flannelboard each time.

Sung to: "Frere Jacques"

See the pretzels, see the pretzels,

In a row, in a row.

Can you guess how many?

I think we should count them.

Here we go, here we go.

   (Count pretzels.)

Lynn Cummisford
Waukesha, WI

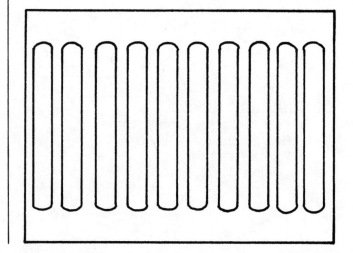

Pretzel Math

Give each child a paper cup with ten stick pretzels in it. Ask the children to each take out four pretzels and place them in a row. Then have them each take out two more pretzels and place those by the first ones. How many pretzels do they each have? Continue to have the children add or subtract pretzels and count the totals.

Variation: Instead of adding and subtracting, just have the children count out specific numbers of pretzels.

Big and Little

Set out a bowl of large and small pretzel twists. Let the children take turns sorting the pretzels by size.

PRETZELS

Pretzel Shapes

Have the children pretend to be pretzels. Ask them to curl themselves into as many different shapes as they can.

I Love Pretzels

Sung to: "Alouette"

I love pretzels, I love pretzels,
I love pretzels, thick and thin.
I love pretzels in my tum,
I love pretzels, yum, yum, yum.
In my tum, yum, yum, yum, – oh,
I love pretzels, I love pretzels,
I love pretzels, thick and thin.

Gayle Bittinger

Pretzel and Cheese Snacks

Give each child a plate with several stick pretzels and cubes of cheese on it. Let the children spear their cheese cubes with their pretzels, then eat them.

Making Pretzels

Dissolve 1 package yeast in 1½ cups of warm water (105-115 degrees) and add ½ teaspoon sugar. Add 4½ cups flour and knead for 6 minutes. Let the dough rise, covered, in a greased bowl until double in size. Divide the dough into 12 pieces and let the children roll them into long sticks. Then let them twist the dough into shapes or letters. Blend together one egg yolk and 2 tablespoons water and have the children brush some of the mixture on their pretzels. Next, let them sprinkle on some coarse salt or sesame seeds. Help the children place their pretzels on a cookie sheet. Bake at 450 degrees for 12 minutes. If desired, keep the pretzels warm in a crock pot set on low. Makes 12 giant pretzels.

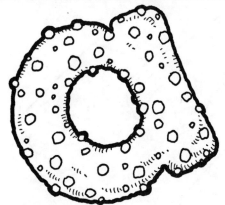

Children's Books:
• *Pretzel*, Margaret Rey, (Harper, 1944).

Contributors:
Lynn Cummisford, Waukesha, WI

Drawing Rainbows

Give the children pieces of white construction paper and crayons with the papers removed. Have the children use the sides of their crayons to draw arcs on their papers. If you want the children to make "authentic" rainbows, have them start at the tops of their papers with red arcs and then under them draw orange, yellow, green, blue and purple arcs, in that order.

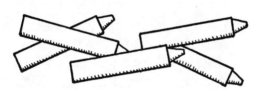

Variation: Tape three to five crayons or felt-tip markers together and let the children take turns drawing arcs with them. Or soak pieces of colored chalk in water for about five minutes, then let the children use the sides of the chalk to draw rainbows.

Tissue Paper Rainbows

Set out several colors of tissue paper, paint brushes, small bowls of liquid starch and pieces of white construction paper. Let each child choose a piece of tissue paper and tear it into small pieces. Then have the child brush an arc of liquid starch on his or her paper and press the tissue pieces on top of the starch. Let the children follow the same procedure to make other colored tissue paper arcs beneath their first ones.

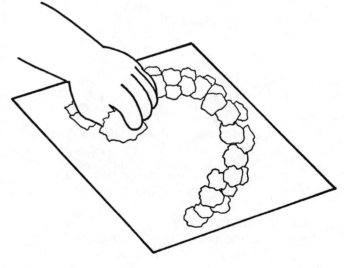

Rainbow Colors

Cut a purple, a blue, a green, a yellow, an orange and a red arc out of felt. Make each arc slightly larger than the one before it so that the purple arc is the smallest and the red arc is the largest. Then sing the song below and let the children place the appropriate colored arcs, one at a time, on a flannelboard to create a rainbow.

Sung to: "Hush, Little Baby"

Rainbow purple, rainbow blue,
Rainbow green and yellow too.
Rainbow orange, rainbow red,
Rainbow smiling overhead.

Come and count the colors with me,
How many colors can you see?
One, two, three, up to green,
Four, five, six colors can be seen.

Rainbow purple, rainbow blue,
Rainbow green and yellow too.
Rainbow orange, rainbow red,
Rainbow smiling overhead.

Jean Warren

Making Rainbows

On a sunny day use a garden hose to spray a fine mist of water across the sun's rays. Have the children stand with their backs to the sun and look for a rainbow in the mist. Name the rainbow colors with the children (red, orange, yellow, green, blue and purple). Explain that sunlight contains all these colors mixed together and when it hits the water from the garden hose (or raindrops in the sky), all the colors are separated.

Variation: Place a small mirror in a glass of water and tilt it against the side of the glass. Then stand the glass in a window, in direct sunlight, so that the mirror reflects a rainbow on a wall.

Rainbow Story

Have the children fill in the blanks as you read this open-ended story out loud.

I see a rainbow.

It is more colorful than _____ .

My favorite rainbow color is _____ .

If I look under the rainbow, I will find _____ .

If I had a rainbow, I would _____ .

If I had two rainbows, I would give one to _____ .

Jean Warren

Rainbow Game

Cut a red, an orange, a yellow, a green, a blue and a purple half-circle out of construction paper. Make each half-circle slightly smaller than the one before it. Set out the colorful half-circles and let the children take turns arranging them from large to small, one on top of the other, to make a rainbow.

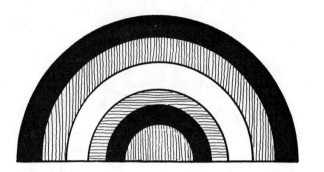

Rainbow Over the Waterfall

Help the children make up hand movements, like the ones hula dancers use, to represent each of these words: rainbow, waterfall, tree, mountain, sea, flowers, bee, dancers, me. Then recite the poem below and let the children use their hand movements to act out the words.

Rainbow over the waterfall,
Rainbow over the tree,
Rainbow over the mountain,
Rainbow over the sea.

Rainbow over the flowers,
Rainbow over the bee,
Rainbow over the dancers,
Rainbow over me!

Jean Warren

Rainbow Song
Sung to: "Twinkle, Twinkle, Little Star"

When the rain falls from the sky,
   (Flutter fingers downward.)
Don't forget to look up high.
   (Cup hand above eyes and look up.)
If the sun is shining there,
   (Make a circle with arms above head.)
You may find a rainbow fair.
   (Sweep arms in an arc above head.)
Red, orange, yellow, green and blue,
And you'll see there's purple too.

Vicki Claybrook
Kennewick, WA

Rainbow Fruit Salad

Make a fruit salad that contains all the colors of the rainbow. Use strawberries, oranges, pineapple, green grapes, blueberries and purple plums. Serve with vanilla yogurt, if desired.

Rainbow Vegetables

Let the children snack on a rainbow of colors of vegetables, such as red tomatoes; orange carrots; yellow, red and green peppers; green celery and broccoli and purple cabbage. If desired, make a simple vegetable dip by combining cottage cheese and ranch dressing. Mix to taste.

Children's Books:

- *Skyfire*, Frank Asch, (Prentice Hall, 1984).
- *Planting a Rainbow*, Lois Ehlert, (Harcourt, 1988).
- *A Rainbow of My Own*, Don Freeman, (Viking, 1966).

Wooden Robots

Set out pieces of scrap wood, nails, hammers, buttons, jar lids and wood glue. Let the children use the materials to build robots. Encourage them to experiment with arranging the wood pieces in different ways before nailing or gluing them together. When the children have finished, let them paint their robots any color they wish.

Egg Carton Robots

Give each child five egg cups cut out of a cardboard egg carton. Have the children glue their egg cups together in robot shapes as shown. Let them decorate their robots by gluing on scraps of aluminum foil or foil wrapping paper. Then let them add plastic moving eyes and pipe cleaner arms.

Variation: Instead of gluing on foil scraps, let the children paint their robots gray.

Rectangular Robots

Cut various sizes of rectangles out of different colors and kinds of paper. Give each child a piece of construction paper and set out the rectangles. Let the children arrange and glue the rectangles on their papers to look like robots. Have them add additional features with felt-tip markers, if desired.

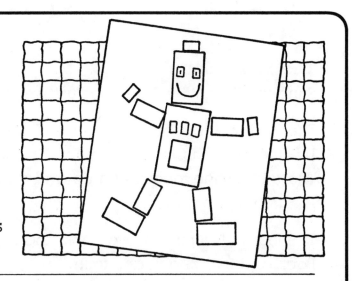

Robot Jobs

Robots are machines that have been made and programmed to perform jobs that people usually do. Ask the children to name jobs they would like to have a robot do for them.

Robot Pairs

On a pair of index cards, draw matching pictures of a simple robot. On four or five other pairs of index cards, draw slightly different matching robot pictures. Mix up the cards and let the children find the robot pairs.

The Robot Song

Sung to: "The Wheels on the Bus"

The arms of the robot swing up and down,
Up and down, up and down.
The arms of the robot swing up and down,
All around the room.

The legs of the robot move back and forth,
Back and forth, back and forth.
The legs of the robot move back and forth,
All around the room.

The head of the robot turns side to side,
Side to side, side to side.
The head of the robot turns side to side,
All around the room.

The buttons on the robot blink on and off,
On and off, on and off.
The buttons on the robot blink on and off,
All around the room.

The voice of the robot says beep, beep, beep,
Beep, beep, beep; beep, beep, beep.
The voice of the robot says beep, beep, beep,
All around the room.

Let the children act out the movements
described as they sing the song.

Serena K. Butch
Schenectady, NY

I'm a Little Robot

Sung to: "I'm a Little Teapot"

I'm a little robot, short and strong.
Here are my handles, just turn me on.
When I get all warmed up, watch me go,
Sometimes fast and sometimes slow.

Jean Warren

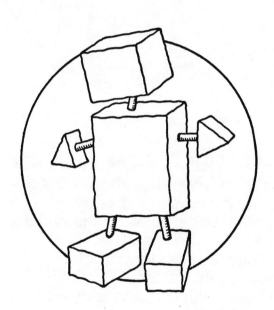

Cheese Robots

At snacktime cut cheese into different sized chunks. Then provide the children with toothpicks and let them put the chunks together to create "cheese robots."

Note: Have the children remove the toothpicks before eating their cheese robots.

Children's Books:
- *Space Case*, James Marshall, (Dial, 1980).
- *Jed's Junior Space Control*, Jean Marzollo, (Dial, 1982).

Contributors:
Ellen Javernick, Loveland, CO
Susan M. Paprocki, Northbrook, IL
Kristine Wagoner, Federal Way, WA

SCARECROWS

Hanging Scarecrows

Give each child a small paper bag. Have the children stuff their bags with crumpled sheets of newspaper. Close each bag with a twist tie or a piece of yarn. Cut eye, nose and mouth shapes out of construction paper. Have the children hold their bags so that the twist ties are at the bottom. Then let them glue the eye, nose and mouth shapes of their choice on their bags. Tape each child's bag to the top of a coat hanger. Put an old shirt or coat on each hanger, add hats, if desired, and the scarecrows are ready to hang.

Scarecrow Pictures

Cut shirt and pants shapes out of fabric and face shapes out of construction paper. Let the children glue the shapes on pieces of construction paper to make scarecrows. Let them add facial features with crayons, if desired. Set out 1-inch pieces of straw. Let the children glue the straw pieces around the edges of their scarecrows.

Variation: Use 1-inch pieces of yellow yarn instead of straw.

Five Stuffed Scarecrows

Let the children take turns acting
out the movements as you recite
the following poem:

Five stuffed scarecrows in the corn rows,

> (Stand straight and tall.)

The first one said, "Go away, crows!"

> (Wave arms.)

The second one said, "I am very small."

> (Crouch down low.)

The third one said, "I am standing tall."

> (Stand on tiptoe.)

The fourth one said, "On my head I wear a hat."

> (Put pretend hat on head.)

The fifth one said, "By my feet runs a cat."

> (Look down.)

Five stuffed scarecrows in the corn rows,

> (Stand straight and tall.)

Moving left and right as the autumn wind blows.

> (Sway back and forth.)

Rita Graef
New Port Richey, FL

SCARECROWS

By the Old Barn Door

Ask each child to hold up five fingers. As you recite the poem below, have the children put their fingers down, one at a time.

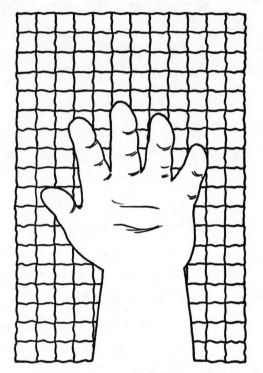

Five little scarecrows by the old barn door,
One went home and then there were four.

Four little scarecrows by the old oak tree,
One went home and then there were three.

Three little scarecrows with nothing to do,
One went home and then there were two.

Two little scarecrows out in the sun,
One went home and then there was one.

One little scarecrow all alone through the day,
He scared the black crows and they all flew away.

Jean Warren

Corn Snacks

Talk with the children about why farmers put scarecrows in their fields. Explain that one reason is to keep crows and other birds from eating the corn as it's growing on the stalks. Then serve the children a corn snack such as corn on the cob, popcorn, cornflakes or cornbread.

The Funny Scarecrow

Sung to: "The Muffin Man"

Have you seen the funny scarecrow,
The funny scarecrow, the funny
  scarecrow?
Have you seen the funny scarecrow,
Who guards our corn field?

He scares away the big black birds,
The big black birds, the big black
  birds.
He scares away the big black birds,
Who eat up all our corn.

Watch him wave his scary arms,
His scary arms, his scary arms.
Watch him wave his scary arms,
When the wind blows by.

Jean Warren

Children's Books:
- *Even the Moose Won't Listen to Me*,
  Martha Alexander, (Dial, 1988).
- *Scarebird*, Sid Fleischman,
  (Greenwillow, 1988).
- *The Little Old Lady Who Was Not Afraid
  of Anything*, Linda Williams, (Harper, 1986).

Scarecrow, Scarecrow

Cut pictures from magazines (or draw your own) of fall objects such as a pumpkin, a cornstalk, a full moon, a haystack and some colorful autumn leaves. Have the children sit in a circle. Pick one child to be the Scarecrow, then recite the first two lines of the following poem. Stop and hold up one of the pictures. Ask the Scarecrow to name the object. Then have all the children recite the last three lines of the poem, inserting the name of the object where indicated. Repeat until each child has had a turn being the Scarecrow.

Scarecrow, Scarecrow, what do you see,
Alone at night by the old oak tree?
(Name of object), (name of object),
That's what (he/she) sees,
Alone at night by the old oak tree.

Jean Warren

Contributors:
Rita Graef, New Port Richey, FL

SHAMROCKS

Shamrock Collages

Set out a variety of green items such as green fabric scraps, green ribbon, green plastic grass, green noodles and green buttons. Give each child a green construction paper shamrock shape. Then let the children choose green items to glue on their shamrocks to make collages.

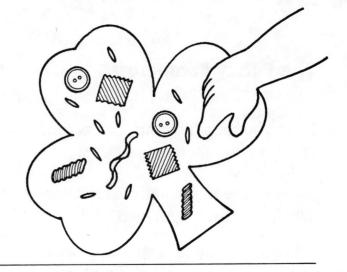

Glittering Shamrocks

Set out green tempera paint, brushes and glitter. Give each child three white paper plates. Let the children paint their paper plates green. Then have them sprinkle glitter over the paint. When the paint has dried, staple each child's plates together and attach a green construction paper stem shape to make a shamrock.

Giant Shamrock Puzzle

Cut a giant shamrock shape out of posterboard. Then cut the shape into puzzle pieces, one piece for each child. Mark the back of each puzzle piece with a felt-tip marker. Set out small squares of green construction paper or tissue paper, glue and cotton swabs. Give each child a puzzle piece. Have the children use the cotton swabs to spread glue all over the unmarked sides of their puzzle pieces. Then have them cover the glue with the green paper squares to create mosaic designs. After the glue has dried, put the shamrock puzzle together on a wall or bulletin board.

Sprouting Shamrocks

Plan to do this activity about one week before green shamrocks are needed. Cut a shamrock shape for each child out of terry cloth. Have the children place their shamrocks in aluminum pie tins and add a little water. Then let them sprinkle alfalfa seeds all over their shapes. Place the pie tins in a sunny spot and have the children add water regularly to keep the shapes moist. Let them observe during the week as the seeds sprout and turn their shamrocks green.

SHAMROCKS

Shamrock Folder Game

On the inside of a file folder draw the outlines of eight shamrocks and write a different number inside each one. Cover the folder with clear self-stick paper. Draw matching shamrock shapes on posterboard, add corresponding numbers of dots, cover the shapes with clear self-stick paper and cut them out. To play the game, give a child the shamrock cutouts and the file folder. Let the child count the number of dots on the cutouts

and place them on top of the matching numbered shamrocks on the file folder.

Shamrock Search

Cut shamrock shapes out of green felt and hide them around the room. Then let the children search for the shapes while singing the song below. Each time they find a shamrock, have them place it on a flannelboard and take a bow. When all the shamrocks have been found, count them together with the children.

Sung to: "The Farmer in the Dell"

Let's look for shamrocks now,
Let's look for shamrocks now,
And when we find a bright green one,
Then we can take a bow!

Jean Warren

Shamrock Number Matching

Give each child a piece of light green construction paper with numbers from 1 to 6 written on it in a random order and six shamrock stickers numbered from 1 to 6. Let the children identify the numbers on their stickers and attach them to their papers next to the corresponding numbers.

Children's Books:
- *St. Patrick's Day in the Morning*, Eve Bunting, (Houghton Mifflin, 1980).
- *Fin M'Coul*, Tomie DePaola, (Holiday, 1988).

Shamrock Sandwiches

Let the children help make open-faced sandwiches by spreading soft cream cheese on slices of whole-wheat bread. Let each child in turn place an open shamrock-shaped cookie cutter on top of his or her sandwich and fill it with alfalfa sprouts. Then have the child remove the cookie cutter to reveal a green sprout shamrock on top of the cheese.

Contributors:
Joleen Meier, Marietta, GA
Karen Seehusan, Fort Dodge, IA

SHELLS

Where to Get Shells

Shells can often be purchased inexpensively at import stores or craft shops. Or check with local fish markets to see if they will let you have discarded shells or shell pieces.

Shell Collages

Set out small shells or shell pieces. Give each child a cardboard square or a paper plate. Let the children glue the shells on their squares or plates to make shell collages.

Shell Display

Display a variety of sizes and types of shells on a table. Add one or two books about shells and several magnifying glasses. Encourage the children to touch the shells, to examine them with the magnifying glasses and to describe how the shells look and feel. Have them hold the shells up to their ears. What do they hear?

Shells Are Houses

Explain to the children that seashells are houses for the animals that live inside them. What kinds of houses do other animals live in? What kinds of houses do people live in?

Sorting Shells

Have the children sit in a circle. Give them shells to pass around. Ask them to describe the different sizes, textures, shapes and colors of the shells. Then let them sort the shells into groups according to size (big and little), texture (smooth and rough), shape or color.

Shell Match-Ups

On a table or the floor, set out pairs of different kinds of shells in a random order. Let the children take turns selecting a shell and finding its match.

Shells, Shells, Shells
Sung to: "Jingle Bells"

Giant shells, tiny shells,
Shells wherever I look.
There are so very many shells,
I could write a book.
Rainbow shells, purple shells,
Shells that curve around.
I can see the beauty here
Just lying on the ground.

Jean Warren

Silly Sally
Sung to: "Mary Had a Little Lamb"

Silly Sally sells seashells,
Sells seashells, sells seashells.
Silly Sally sells seashells
Down at the seashore.

Karen Brown
Siloam Springs, AR

Shell Game

Hide an object under one of three shells lined up in a row. Then move the shells around and have the children guess which shell the object is hidden under.

Shell Salads

Cook pasta shells according to the package directions. Let cool. Set out relish and cubes of cheese. Chop vegetables, such as celery, onions, peppers and olives, and place them in separate containers. Give each child a small bowl with some pasta and a spoonful of mayonnaise in it. Let the children add small amounts of the relish, cheese cubes and chopped vegetables as they like. Then have them stir up their shell salads and eat.

Children's Books:
- *When the Tide Is Low,* Joanna Cole, (Lothrop, 1985).
- *One Morning in Maine,* Robert McCloskey, (Puffin, 1952).
- *Biggest House in World,* Leo Lionni, (Knopf, 1987).

Contributors:
Karen Brown, Siloam Springs, AR
Dawn Picollelli, Wilmington, DE

SHOES

Shoe Rubbings

Set out several fairly new athletic shoes. (Use the children's shoes or ones you have on hand.) Let the children place pieces of white paper over the soles of the shoes and rub across their papers with crayons.

Shoe Matching

Place five shoeboxes on a table or on the floor. Mix up five pairs of shoes and put them in a pile. Let the children find the matching pairs of shoes and place one pair in each of the shoeboxes.

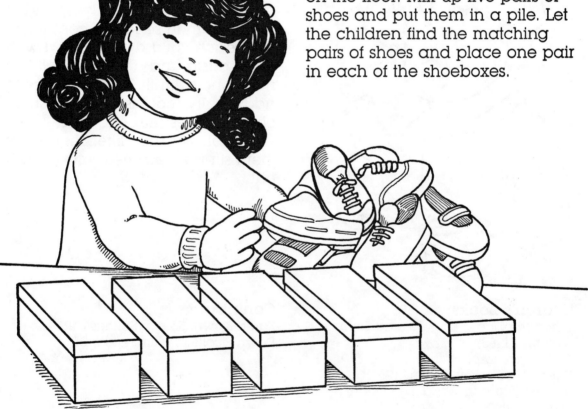

Shoe Fasteners

Collect several pairs of shoes, with different kinds of fasteners such as laces, buckles, snaps, zippers or Velcro fastening tape. Let the children try on the different kinds of shoes and practice fastening and unfastening them.

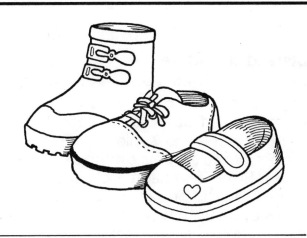

Shoe Sort

Gather together a collection of ten to fifteen pairs of shoes. Have the children sort the shoes by color, size, texture, seasonal use or fasteners.

Shoe Talk

Collect five or six kinds of shoes that people wear to do different activities. Some examples would be thongs, rubber boots, hiking boots, tennis shoes and slippers. Show each of the shoes to the children and ask them to describe what a person wearing the shoes might be doing.

Listening Game

Show the children several pairs of shoes that make different sounds when walked across a tile floor, such as tennis shoes, high heels, rubber boots, slippers and tap shoes. Have the children close their eyes. Then slip one of the pairs of shoes on your hands and walk them across a tile floor or a tabletop. Ask the children to guess which pair of shoes it is. Continue with the remaining shoes.

Shoe Store

Set up a Shoe Store in a corner of the room. Include two or three chairs, a ruler for measuring foot sizes (or a foot measuring stick from a shoe store, if possible) and several pairs of shoes in boxes. Let the children take turns being the customer and the salesperson.

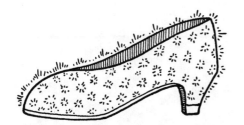

Glitter Shoes

Decorate old pairs of men's and women's shoes with red glitter. Let the children clomp around in them for special occasions.

Shoes

Sung to: "Farmer in the Dell"

We all wear shoes,
We all wear shoes.
To keep our feet so warm and clean,
We all wear shoes.

We wear them when we run,
We wear them when we jump.
We wear them when we go outside,
We all wear shoes.

We wear them when it rains,
We wear them when it snows.
We wear them when the sun is out,
We all wear shoes.

Lisa A. Thomas
Port Carbon, PA

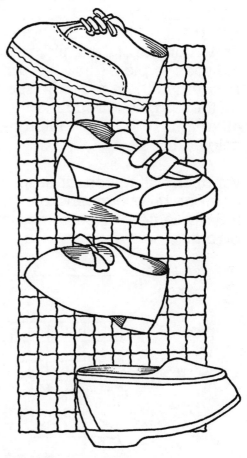

Children's Books:
- *Big Shoe, Little Shoe*, Denys Cazet, (Bradbury, 1984).
- *New Blue Shoes*, Eve Rice, (Viking, 1979).
- *Shoes*, Elizabeth Winthrop, (Bradbury, 1984).

Contributors:
Betty Silkunas, Lansdale, PA

Sponge-Print Trees

Make paint pads by folding paper towels in half, placing them in shallow containers and pouring on small amounts of red, orange and yellow tempera paints. Cut sponges into small pieces. Give each child a piece of construction paper with a tree trunk shape drawn on it. Let the children dip the sponge pieces into the paint. Then have them press the sponges on their papers all around the tops of the trunks to make autumn-colored trees.

Variation: Let the children sponge-paint green evergreens, green and red apple trees or pink trees in bloom.

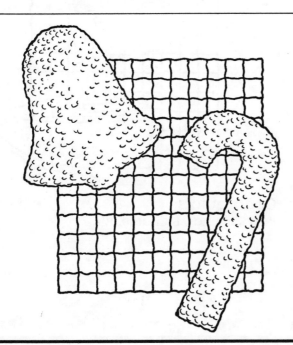

Sponge-Print Art

Cut sponges into various seasonal or holiday shapes. Make paint pads by adding small amounts of paint to folded paper towels in shallow containers. Cover a large table with butcher paper. Let the children lightly press the sponge shapes on the paint pads, then print with them on the butcher paper.

Sniffing Sponges

Place several sponges on a tray. Add a drop of a different smelling liquid to each sponge. Try such liquids as vanilla extract, coconut extract, vinegar, lemon juice and perfume. Let the children take turns sniffing the sponges and describing how they smell.

Sponge Puppets

Cut sponges into 1½- by 2½-inch pieces. Make a slit in one of the narrow ends of each sponge piece with a sharp knife. (Make sure each slit is large enough to fit over a finger.) Decorate the sponges with felt features and yarn hair. Slip the sponges on your fingers. Use the sponge puppets while telling stories or singing songs.

SPONGES

Sponge Games

Let the children do the following activities:

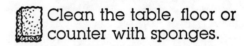 Clean the table, floor or counter with sponges.

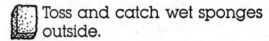 Toss and catch wet sponges outside.

 Squeeze the water out of wet sponges (outside or over a sink or a dishpan).

Use sponges as building blocks.

Sorting Sponges

Cut different colors of sponges into various shapes and sizes. Let the children take turns sorting the sponge pieces by shape, color or size.

Sponge Puzzles

Make simple puzzles by using a sharp knife to cut a different shape out of each of several large flat sponges. Set out both pieces from each puzzle and let the children take turns putting them together and taking them apart.

French Fry Counter

Cut a yellow sponge into long skinny rectangles to use as "French fries." Let the children take turns counting how many fries will fit into a large cardboard French fry holder. Or let them use the fries and holder for creative play.

Little Yellow Sponge

Sung to: "If You're Happy and You Know It"

Oh, I wish I had a little yellow sponge,
Oh, that is what I'd truly like to say.
For if I had a little sponge, a little yellow sponge,
I could clean and clean and clean and clean all day.

First I'd wipe across all the counters,
Then across the tables nice and slow.
Next I'd tackle all the walls, all the great big dirty walls,
Then you'd really see my little sponge go!

Jean Warren

Children's Books:
- *The Very Hungry Caterpillar,* Eric Carle, (Putnam, 1981).
- *Swimmy,* Leo Lionni, (Knopf, 1987).

Contributors:
Betty Lou Pitts, Victoria, TX
Carole Sick, Louisville, KY

Mosaic Pictures

Cut tiny squares out of various colors of construction paper. Set out the squares, glue, cotton swabs and pieces of construction paper. Have the children use the cotton swabs to spread glue on the construction paper. Then let them place the small squares on their papers to create simple scenes.

Square Art

Cut different sizes of squares out of a variety of kinds of paper such as construction paper, wrapping paper, tissue paper and newspaper. Put the paper squares in a box. Give each child a piece of construction paper cut into a square. Let the children select squares from the box to arrange and glue on their construction paper squares.

Animal Squares

Have the children glue construction paper squares to Popsicle sticks. Let them use felt-tip markers, construction paper scraps, fabric scraps, ribbon and yarn to create animal faces on their squares.

Square Puppets

For each child cut one large square, four small squares, two 4-inch strips and two 6-inch strips out of construction paper. Give each child his or her shapes. Show the children how to fold the strips accordion-style. Have them glue the shorter strips to their large squares for arms and the longer ones for legs. Let them attach the small squares to the ends of the folded paper strips for hands and feet. Have the children draw faces on their large squares. Then glue on Popsicle stick handles to complete the puppets.

Sally the Square

Have the children hold their Square Puppets and their Animal Squares from the previous activities. Ask the children to name the kinds of animal puppets they have made and to substitute those names for the animal names in the following poem:

When Sally the Square
Went to the fair,
She was all alone and blue.
Then she found a square cat
To be her friend,
And now the squares are two.

When Sally the Square
Went to the fair,
She was all alone, you see.
But she found a square cat
And then a square pig,
And now the squares are three.

When Sally the Square
Went to the fair,
She wanted to see more.
She found a square cat,
A square pig, then a duck,
And now the squares are four.

Jean Woods
Tulsa, OK

Shapes From Squares

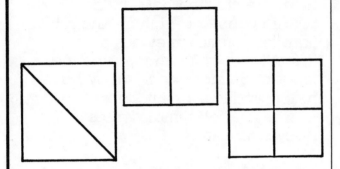

Give each child three 6-inch squares. Show the children how to fold and cut one of their squares into two triangles. Then show them how to cut their other two squares into two rectangles and four smaller squares, respectively.

I Spy a Square

Have the children sit in a circle in the middle of the room. Let them glance around the room as you call attention to different square objects. Then let one child begin by saying, "I spy with my little eye something square." Have the other children try guessing what the object is. When a player guesses correctly, let him or her have the next turn.

Sequencing Squares

Cut different sized squares out of construction paper. Give the children the squares and let them take turns putting them in order from smallest to largest.

Square Sandwiches

Cut slices of cheese, cold cuts, tomatoes and bread into squares of the same size. Set out butter or margarine, plastic knives and paper plates. Let the children put the square sandwich makings of their choice on the plates. Help them spread butter on their bread slices. Then let them put their square sandwiches together. Serve boxes of juice with the sandwiches, if desired.

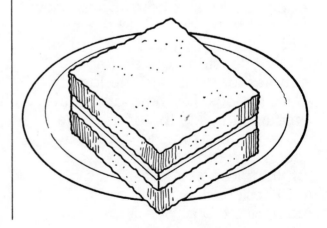

Square Shape Song

Give the children square shapes
cut out of construction paper. Let
them use the shapes to act out the
movements in the following song:

Sung to: "Twinkle, Twinkle, Little Star"

Put your square shape in the air,
Hold it high and keep it there.
Put your square shape on your back,
Now please lay it on your lap.
Put your square shape on your toes,
Now please hold it by your nose.

Hold your square shape in your hand,
Now will everyone please stand.
Wave your square shape at the door,
Now please lay it on the floor.
Hold your square shape and jump, jump, jump,
Now throw your square shape way, way up.

Trish Peckham
Raleigh, NC

Children's Books:
- *Boxes! Boxes!*, Everett Fischer,
  (Viking, 1984).
- *Look Around!*, Everett Fischer,
  (Puffin, 1987).
- *Shapes*, Lynn Kightley,
  (Little Brown, 1986).

Contributors:
Trish Peckham, Raleigh, NC

STICKERS

Sticker Art

Let the children fingerpaint with blue paint on sheets of paper. Allow the paint to dry. Then give the children butterfly or boat stickers to attach to their painted papers.

Variation: Use green fingerpaint and fish or flower stickers. Or use black fingerpaint and star stickers.

Bouncing Ball Book

Cut small pictures out of magazines and trim them to fit in the pages of a wing-type wallet photo holder. Attach a circle sticker to each picture. Put two of the pictures in each of the photo holder pages, picture sides out. Let the children tell the story of the "bouncing ball" as it moves from page to page.

Sticker Puppets

Make simple puppets by attaching stickers to the ends of tongue depressors. If a sticker is larger than the tongue depressor, place a plain piece of paper behind it and trim to the sticker shape. Let the children use the puppets while reciting favorite rhymes or singing songs.

Variation: Make puppets by attaching stickers to your fingers.

Color Sticker Song

Give each child a red, a blue, a yellow or a green self-stick dot to put on a finger. Then sing the song below and have the children with the appropriate color of sticker do the action described in that verse.

Sung to: "If You're Happy and You Know It"

If you have a yellow sticker, clap your hands,
If you have a yellow sticker, clap your hands.
If your sticker's really yellow,
Then you are a lucky fellow.
If you have a yellow sticker, clap your hands.

If you have a green sticker, make a face,
If you have a green sticker, make a face.
If your sticker's really green,
Then make a face that's oh, so mean.
If you have a green sticker, make a face.

If you have a red sticker, say "Hurray!"
If you have a red sticker, say "Hurray!"
If your sticker's really red,
Then say "Hurray!" and pat your head.
If you have a red sticker, say "Hurray!"

If you have a blue sticker, turn around,
If you have a blue sticker, turn around.
If your sticker's really blue,
Then turn around and touch your shoe.
If you have a blue sticker, turn around.

Jean Warren

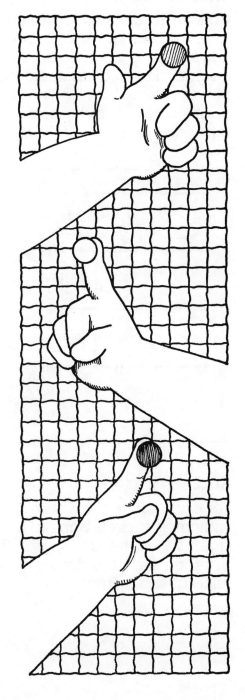

STICKERS

Sticker Sorting

Collect an assortment of stickers in three different categories such as flowers, birds and bears. Attach each sticker to a small index card. Mix up the cards and let the children sort them by category into three different containers.

Sticker Lotto

Cut a 9-inch square out of posterboard. Divide it into nine 3- by 3-inch sections and put a different sticker in each one. Then cut nine 3- by 3-inch cards out of posterboard and put corresponding stickers on them. Have the children play lotto by matching the stickers on the cards to the stickers in the sections on the square.

Sticker Straws

For each child attach two matching stickers back-to-back around a straw. Let the children use their straws to drink milk or juice at snacktime.

Sticker Matching

Cut a large donut shape out of posterboard. Use a felt-tip marker to divide the donut into ten sections. Attach matching stickers on the opposite sides of each dividing line. Cut out the sections. Let the children take turns piecing the donut together by matching the stickers.

Sticker Dominoes

Divide each of 21 small index cards with a line. Collect seven each of six different stickers such as a bear, a flower, a cat, a rainbow, a duck and a clown. Attach two stickers on each of the 21 cards, using these combinations: bear-bear, bear-flower, bear-cat, bear-rainbow, bear-duck, bear-clown; flower-flower, flower-cat, flower-rainbow, flower-duck, flower-clown; cat-cat, cat-rainbow, cat-duck, cat-clown; rainbow-rainbow, rainbow-duck, rainbow-clown; duck-duck, duck-clown; clown-clown. Let the children use the cards to play dominoes.

Children's Books:
- *Maggie B*, Irene Hunt, (Macmillan, 1975).
- *A Reason for a Flower*, Ruth Heller, (Putnam, 1983).
- *The Sky Is Full of Stars*, Franklyn Branley, (Harper, 1981).

Contributors:
Kathleen Tobey, Griffith, IN

Stringing Straws

Let the children cut straws into 1- to 2-inch sections. Give each child an 18-inch piece of yarn with a straw section tied to one end and the other end taped to make a "needle." Have the children string their straw sections on their pieces of yarn. Tie the ends of each child's yarn piece together to make a necklace.

Straw Evergreens

Set out glue in shallow containers and straws cut into a variety of lengths. Give each child a piece of construction paper with a vertical line drawn on it. Let the children dip the straw pieces into the glue and place them at an angle on both sides of their vertical lines to create straw "evergreen trees."

Straw Painting

Put pieces of white construction paper and shallow containers of tempera paint on a table. Let the children dip straws into the paint and drizzle it on the pieces of paper. Then let them gently blow through the straws to scatter the paint all over the papers. (Poke small holes in the tops of the straws to prevent the children from accidentally drinking the paint.)

Straw Birthday Candles

Cut straws into 3-inch sections. Let the children use playdough to make birthday cakes. Have them decorate their cakes with the straw "candles." Together, count the number of candles on each child's cake.

Tossing Game

Cut the centers out of small plastic lids, leaving just the rims. Give each child a straw and a lid rim. Have each child hold his or her straw in one hand, toss up the lid with the other hand and try to catch it on the straw.

Magic Straws

Let the children use straws as props for creative dramatics. The straws could become such things as batons, fishing poles, pencils, paint brushes, drumsticks or flashlights. Then sing the song below and have the children act out the movements and take turns filling in the blank.

Sung to: "This Old Man"

Magic straw, see it here,
Watch it vanish, then appear.
Look, a _____ is in my hand,
This magic straw is really grand!

Jean Warren

Sipping Through Straws

At snacktime let the children use straws to sip orange juice or milk. Or make a special sipping treat such as Cantaloupe Coolers.

Cantaloupe Coolers – Process 1 cup cantaloupe chunks, ¼ cup unsweetened frozen apple juice concentrate and 1 cup milk in a blender for a foamy drink. Makes 4 small servings.

Decorated Straws

Cut simple seasonal shapes, such as fall leaves or spring butterflies, out of construction paper. Cut two slits, about 1-inch apart, in the middle of each shape. Slip the shapes over straws for decorations.

Children's Books:
- *Arthur's Birthday,* Marc Brown, (Little Brown, 1989).
- *If You Give a Mouse a Cookie,* Laura Numeroff, (Harper, 1985).

Contributors:
Betty Silkunas, Lansdale, PA

TONGUE DEPRESSORS

Log Cabins

Give each child four tongue depressors, a brown construction paper roof shape and a piece of construction paper. Let the children color their tongue depressors with brown crayons before gluing them in log cabin shapes on their papers. Have the children complete their log cabins by gluing on their roof shapes and using crayons to add doors, chimneys and windows.

Hint: Many of the activities in this unit may be done with Popsicle sticks or craft sticks.

Picture Puppets

Cut out magazine pictures of people and animals. Glue each picture to a piece of posterboard and trim around the edges. Then glue a tongue depressor handle to the back of each picture. Give each child a puppet. Ask the children questions and have them answer as if they were their puppet characters.

Stick Puppets

Draw simple faces on the ends of tongue depressors. Add clothing shapes cut from felt or fabric scraps. Glue on pieces of yarn for hair, if desired. Set out the puppets and let the children use them for telling stories.

Counting Sticks

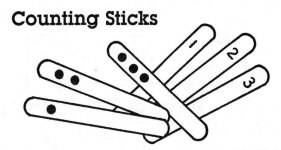

Number ten tongue depressors with sets of dots from 1 to 10. Number ten more tongue depressors with numerals from 1 to 10. Mix up the tongue depressors and let the children take turns finding the matching numbered pairs. Or have them arrange the tongue depressors in order from 1 to 10.

Shape Match-Ups

Cut several large squares out of posterboard. Use tongue depressors to create a different shape on each square. Trace around the tongue depressors with a black felt-tip marker. Set out the squares and a basket of tongue depressors. Let the children select squares and place tongue depressors on top of the tracings to create the shapes shown on the squares.

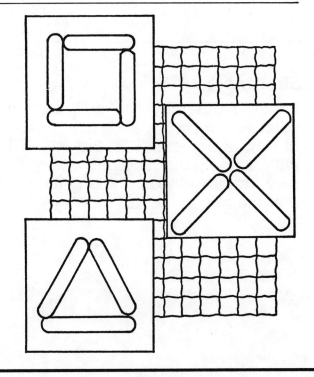

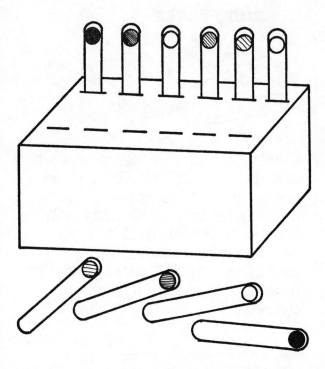

Color Game

Turn a large shoebox upside down and cut two parallel rows of slits in the top. Decorate the ends of one set of tongue depressors with different colored stickers. Decorate the ends of another set of tongue depressors with matching colored stickers. Insert one set of tongue depressors in one of the rows of slits. Then let the children insert matching tongue depressors from the second set in the appropriate slits in the other row.

Variation: Instead of matching colors, have the children match shapes, numbers and dots, or upper- and lower-case alphabet letters.

Streamers

Make streamers by stapling long pieces of crepe paper on the ends of tongue depressors. Let the children hold the streamers while they run or walk fast, making their streamers fly in the air.

Rhythm Sticks

Give each child two tongue depressors to use as rhythm sticks. Let the children tap their sticks while they sing the following song:

Sung to: "The Muffin Man"

Listen while we tap our sticks,
Tap our sticks, tap our sticks.
Listen while we tap our sticks,
We will tap them (number) times.

   (Tap and count.)

Gayle Bittinger

Snacktime Fun

Just for fun, let the children use clean tongue depressors as spoons for eating applesauce or cottage cheese. Or have them use tongue depressors as knives for spreading peanut butter on bread.

Children's Books:
• *My Doctor,* Harlow Rockwell, (Macmillan, 1973).

Contributors:
Nancy Ridgeway, Bradford, PA

Egg Carton Trains

For each child you will need a row of six egg cups cut from a cardboard egg carton and half of a cardboard toilet tissue tube. Have the children turn their egg cup rows upside down and paint them as desired. Then let them paint their toilet tissue tubes black. Allow the paint to dry. Have the children glue their toilet tissue tubes to the tops of the first cups on their egg carton "trains" to complete.

Teddy Bear Train

Hook five or six small cardboard boxes together with yarn. Let the children decorate the boxes with tempera paints or felt-tip markers. Attach a posterboard smokestack shape and a yarn handle to the first box. Have the children put teddy bears or other stuffed animals in the boxes. Let them take turns pulling the boxes by the yarn handle and chugging around the room.

The Train

Sung to: "The Farmer in the Dell"

The train is on the track,
The train is on the track.
Clickity-clack, oh, clickity-clack,
The train is on the track.

The engineer drives the train,
The engineer drives the train.
In the snow and in the rain,
The engineer drives the train.

The caboose is at the back,
The caboose is at the back.
Clickity-clack, oh, clickity-clack,
The caboose is at the back.

Judith Taylor
Burtchet El Dorado, KS

Number Trains

For each child cut out of construction paper one engine shape, five boxcar shapes and one caboose shape. Number the boxcars from 1 to 5. Give each child a set of the train shapes and fifteen stickers. Have the children identify the numbers on their boxcar shapes and attach the corresponding numbers of stickers to them. Ask them to line up their train shapes on a table with their engines first, their boxcars next (in order) and their cabooses last. Tape the shapes together along their sides. Then hang up the number trains or fold them into books.

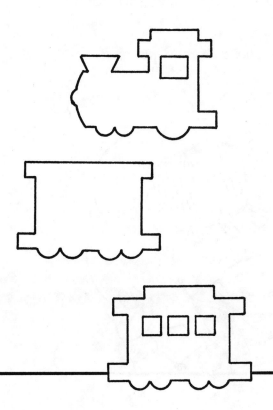

Little Red Train

Have the children sit down and wait in line at an imaginary train station. Chug around the room as everyone recites the poem below. Each time you stop at the station, have the child at the head of the line hook onto the back of your train. Continue until everyone is hooked on and has had a chance to chug around the room.

Little Red Train
Chugging down the track,
First it goes down,
Then it comes back.
Hooking on cars as it goes,
Little Red Train just
Grows and grows.

Jean Warren

Variation: Let each child choose to be a specific type of car such as a boxcar or a circus car. Change the third line of the poem to match the type of car chosen. For example, if a child chooses to be a tank car, change the line to read, "Hooking on a tank car as it goes." Let the last child in line be the caboose.

Choo-Choo Train

Recite the following poem with the children and encourage them to act out the movements.

This is a choo-choo train

    (Bend arms at elbows.)

Puffing down the track.

    (Rotate forearms in rhythm.)

Now it's going forward,

    (Rotate arms forward.)

Now it's going back.

    (Rotate arms backward.)

Now the bell is ringing,

    (Pull pretend bell cord.)

Now the whistle blows.

    (Hold fist near mouth and blow.)

What a lot of noise it makes

    (Cover ears with hands.)

Everywhere it goes!

    (Stretch out arms.)

Author Unknown

The Train

Sung to: "The Farmer in the Dell"

The train is on the track,
The train is on the track.
Clickity-clack, oh, clickity-clack,
The train is on the track.

The engineer drives the train,
The engineer drives the train.
In the snow and in the rain,
The engineer drives the train.

The caboose is at the back,
The caboose is at the back.
Clickity-clack, oh, clickity-clack,
The caboose is at the back.

Judith Taylor
Burtchet El Dorado, KS

The Wheels on the Train

Sung to: "The Wheels on the Bus"

The wheels on the train go clickity-clack,
Clickity-clack, clickity-clack.
The wheels on the train go clickity-clack,
All along the track.

The whistle on the train goes whoo-ee-whoo,
Whoo-ee-whoo, whoo-ee-whoo.
The whistle on the train goes whoo-ee-whoo,
All along the track.

The people on the train go up and down,
Up and down, up and down.
The people on the train go up and down,
All along the track.

The conductor on the train says "All aboard!
All aboard! All aboard!"
The conductor on the train says "All aboard!"
All along the track.

Elizabeth Vollrath
Stevens Pt., WI

Children's Books:
* *Freight Train*, Donald Crews, (Greenwillow, 1978).
* *Trains*, Anne Rockwell, (Dutton, 1988).
* *Train to Grandma's*, Ivan Gantschev, (Picture Book, 1987).

Contributors:
Betty Silkunas, Lansdale, PA

Tissue Paper Turtles

Cut turtle shapes out of light green construction paper. Give the children pieces of green tissue paper to tear into small squares. Have the children brush liquid starch on their turtle shapes. Then let them stick the tissue papers squares all over the starch.

Egg Carton Cup Turtles

Cut small turtle shapes out of green construction paper and cut egg cups out of cardboard egg cartons. Give each child two or three turtle shapes and egg cups. Have the children glue their egg cups on their turtle shapes to represent shells. Then let them paint the egg cups green.

Turtle Shells

Make a "turtle shell" for each child by cutting a head hole in the bottom of a large brown paper bag and two arm holes in the sides of the bag. Let the children paint their turtle shells green. Allow the paint to dry. Help the children put on their shells and encourage them to crawl around the room like turtles.

Extension: Use the turtle shells when reading "The Turtle Walk" poem or singing the "Baby Turtle Song" on page 260.

Color Turtles

Cut turtle shapes out of light green construction paper. Give each child a turtle shape and help the child use crayons to draw one dot on the turtle's back in each of these colors: red, yellow, blue, purple, green, brown, white, orange and black. Then recite the poem below and have the children point to each color on their turtles as you name it.

I can name these colors,
All so very bright,
Red, yellow, blue, purple,
Green, brown and white.
Don't forget the color orange
And the color black,
These are the colors of
The dots upon my turtle's back.

Deborah A. Roessel
Flemington, NJ

Turtle Fingerplay

This is my turtle,
    (Make fist and extend thumb.)
He lives in a shell.
    (Hide thumb in fist.)
He likes his home very well.
He pokes his head out
When he wants to eat,
    (Extend thumb.)
And pulls it back in
When he wants to sleep.
    (Hide thumb in fist.)

Traditional

The Turtle Walk

As you read the poem below, let the children pretend to be turtles crawling very slowly across the floor.

Some folks call me a slowpoke,
But I don't really mind.
'Cause I just like to mosey along
To see what I can find.

I see a lot in the slow lane,
Like every square inch of land.
I marvel at the smallest pebble
And notice each grain of sand.

I'm just a mellow fellow
Who wonders what's all the rush.
So don't tell me to hurry up,
'Cause I'll just answer "Hush!"

So get on down and take it slow
And see what there is to see.
It's really a nifty world,
I know that you will agree.

So stop your pushing and shoving
And filling my heart with woe.
Just creep along at your own pace
And move along with the turtle flow.

Susan M. Paprocki
Northbrook, IL

Quick and Slow

Talk about quick and slow. Ask the children to walk quickly, then slowly. Then have them listen carefully while you ask them to do other things quickly and slowly, such as crawl, talk, skip, clap and jump.

Baby Turtle Song

Sung to: "Mary Had a Little Lamb"

I am just a baby turtle,
Baby turtle, baby turtle.
I am just a baby turtle
Tucked up in my shell.

I will stick my right foot out,
Left foot out, right arm out.
Then I'll stick my left arm out
And go explore the world.

Linda Warren
Newbury Park, CA

Bread Turtles

Use a favorite recipe to make yeast bread and let the children form the dough into turtle shapes before baking. Or use the pretzel recipe on page 207 instead.

Turtle Rounds

Bake banana, carrot or pumpkin bread in 16-ounce tin cans. Slice the bread into rounds about ¼-inch thick. Spread with cream cheese. Place a walnut half on each round. Create a turtle by placing raisins next to the walnut, using one raisin for a head and four raisins for legs.

Variation: Use crackers instead of bread rounds.

Children's Books:
- *Turtle Tale,* Frank Asch, (Dial, 1978).
- *Tortoise and the Hare,* Janet Stevens, (Holiday, 1984).
- *Franklin in the Dark,* Paulette Bourgeois, (Scholastic, 1987).

Contributors:
Penny Larsen, Lincoln, NE
Susan M. Paprocki, Northbrook, IL
Deborah A. Roessel, Flemington, NJ
Linda Warren, Newbury Park, CA

Paper Bag Whales

Have the children stuff small paper bags with crumpled sheets of newspaper. Tie the tops of the bags closed to make whale tails. Let the children paint their paper bag whales gray. Allow the paint to dry. Cut eye shapes out of black construction paper, and have the children glue them to the sides of their whales. Construction paper spout shapes may be added to the tops of the whales, if desired.

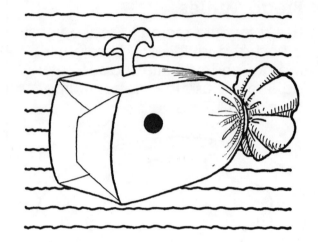

Whale Fingerpainting

Give the children pieces of butcher paper with small amounts of liquid starch on them. Sprinkle blue powder tempera paint on the starch. Let the children fingerpaint on their papers. Have them pretend their hands are whales swimming and playing in the ocean.

Five Big Whales

Cut five whale shapes out of gray or black felt and five spout shapes out of white felt. Lay a piece of blue yarn across a flannelboard to represent the surface of the sea and place the whale shapes beneath it. Then recite the poem below and let the children take turns moving the whale shapes up to the water's surface and placing the spout shapes above the whales' heads.

Five big whales in the sea offshore,
One swam up to spout, and that left four.

Four big whales in the deep blue sea,
One swam up to spout, and that left three.

Three big whales in the sea so blue,
One swam up to spout, and that left two.

Two big whales having lots of fun,
One swam up to spout, and that left one.

One big whale longing for the sun,
It swam up to spout, and that left none.

Elizabeth McKinnon

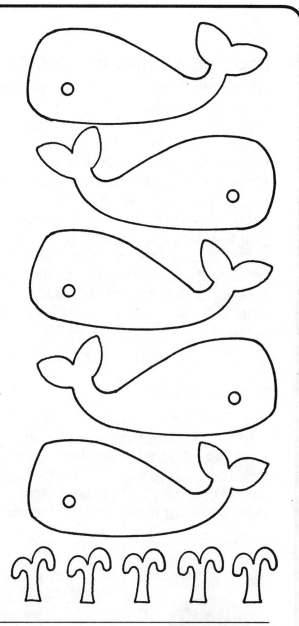

Whale Memory Game

Draw a simple whale shape on each of twelve index cards. Color each pair of whales a different color. Place the cards face down on a table. Have the children take turns turning over two cards at a time, keeping them if they match and turning them face down again if they don't.

Bobbing Whales in the Bottle

Fill a clear plastic 2-liter bottle one-quarter full with water. Add a few drops of blue food coloring. Blow up two small balloons, release most of the air and tie the ends closed. Push the balloons into the bottle and replace the cap securely. When you have finished, you will have an ocean in a bottle with two bobbing whales inside. Let the children hold the bottle on its side and gently rock it back and forth to make the whales swim.

Whale Song

A male humpback whale will often repeat the same song over and over again for several days. Ask the children to listen carefully while you sing a "whale song" composed of three or four different sounds in a row, such as a clap, an "oooh," a "shhh" and a cry. Then have the children repeat the sounds in the order in which you made them.

Whale Moves

Check your library for a recording of whale songs to play for the children. Have them lie on their stomachs on the floor and move like whales while they listen to the recording. Encourage them to raise and lower their legs like tails and to sing their own whale songs.

A Salty Sea Giant

Sung to: "The Muffin Man"

Do you know a giant mammal,
A giant mammal, a giant
      mammal?
Do you know a giant mammal
That lives in the salty sea?

Yes, it is a huge gray whale,
A huge gray whale, a huge gray
      whale.
Yes, it is a huge gray whale,
That lives in the salty sea.

It sprays water out a blowhole,
Out a blowhole, out a blowhole.
It sprays water out a blowhole
And lives in the salty sea.

It swims with a big flat tail,
A big flat tail, a big flat tail.
It swims with a big flat tail
And lives in the salty sea.

Susan A. Miller
Kutztown, PA

Children's Books:
* *Burt Dow: Deep-Water Man*,
  Robert McCloskey, (Viking, 1963).
* *Whale in the Sky*, Anne Siberell,
  (Dutton, 1982).

I'm a Great Big Whale

Sung to: "I'm a Little Teapot"

I'm a great big whale,
Watch me swim.
Here is my blowhole,
      (Point to back of head.)
Here are my fins.
      (Wave hands against body.)
See me flip my tail as down I go,
      (Pretend to dive.)
Then up I come and "Whoosh!"
      I blow.
      (Raise arms above head to form spout.)

Elizabeth McKinnon

Wheel Tracks

Pour small amounts of tempera paint in shallow containers. Give the children toy cars and pieces of construction paper. Let them run the wheels of their cars in the paint, then all across their papers to create designs.

Spinning Art

Cut out various sizes and colors of circles. Make a hole slightly off center in each one. Let the children each select several of the circles and arrange them on top of one another from largest to smallest. Fasten each child's circles together by lining up the holes and inserting a brass paper fastener. Then let the children turn their circles around like wheels to create their own spinning art.

Wheels on Display

Set up a discovery area with a variety of different objects that have wheels. Display such items as toy cars and trucks, a child-sized wheelbarrow, a Lazy Susan, a pair of roller skates and a pizza cutter. Let the children experiment with the wheeled objects, adding others that they find at home or around the room.

Testing Shapes for Wheels

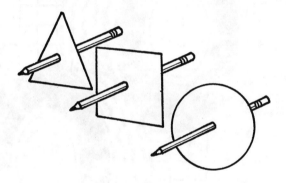

Have the children test different shapes to see which one makes the best wheel. Cut a triangle, a square and a circle out of cardboard. Push a pencil halfway through each shape for an axle. Let the children roll the pencils across a tabletop. Which pencil rolls the easiest? Why? Which shape makes the best wheel?

Round and Round

Cut out magazine pictures of things that have wheels and things that do not. Cover the pictures with clear self-stick paper for durability, if desired. Show the children the pictures, one at a time. If the object has wheels, have the children roll their hands around and around. If the object does not have wheels, have the children shake their heads.

WHEELS

Roll Like Wheels

Ask the children how many ways they can make wheels with their bodies. What parts of their bodies rotate like wheels? Can they rotate more than one body part at the same time? Can they rotate two body parts in different directions at the same time?

Wheels

Sung to: "The Wheels on the Bus"

The wheels on the bus go round and round,
Round and round, round and round.
The wheels on the bus go round and round,
All over town.

The wheels on the car go round and round,
Round and round, round and round.
The wheels on the car go round and round,
All over town.

The wheels on the taxi go round and round,
Round and round, round and round.
The wheels on the taxi go round and round,
All over town.

Continue with similar verses about other vehicles that have wheels.

Adapted Traditional

Watch the Wheels Go Round

Sung to: "My Bonnie Lies Over the Ocean"

I love to play with my cars,
And drive them across the ground.
Sometimes I race them on sidewalks,
And watch the wheels go round.
Round, round, round, round,
I watch the wheels go round, round, round.
Round, round, round, round,
I watch the wheels go round.

Jean Warren

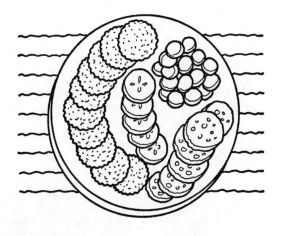

Snack Wheel

Make a snack wheel by placing round crackers, carrot and cucumber rounds and circles cut out of cheese slices on a Lazy Susan. Let the children spin the snack wheel around and serve themselves on round paper plates.

Children's Books:
* *Wheels on the Bus,* Maryann Kovalski, (Little Brown, 1987).
* *Bear's Bicycle,* Emilie McLeod, (Penguin, 1977).
* *Wheels Go Round,* Yvonne Hooker, (Grossett & Dunlap, 1982).

Contributors:
Marjorie S. Debowy, Stony Brook, NY

Wind Art

Take the children outside on a windy day. Give them each a piece of white construction paper with a few drops of tempera paint on it. Have them hold their papers up and let the wind blow the paint into designs.

Windsocks

Give each child an oatmeal box or a salt box (with top and bottom removed) and a piece of construction paper precut to fit around it. Let the children decorate their papers and glue them to the outsides of their boxes. Have the children glue or staple strips of crepe paper around the bottom edges of their boxes. To hang, punch four holes in the top of each box, lace a string knotted at one end through each hole and tie the four loose ends together.

Variation: Have the children attach crepe paper strips around the edges of paper plates. Tie a string through two holes punched in the middle of each plate and hang.

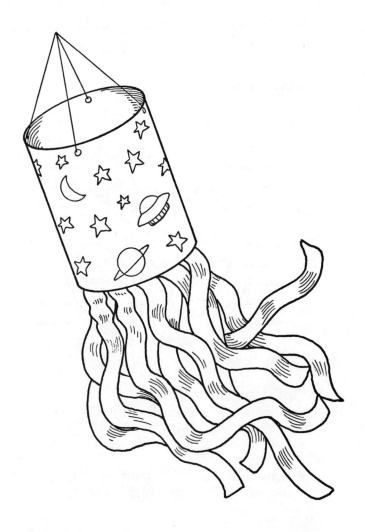

Wind Hummers

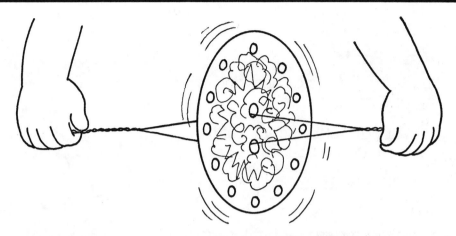

For each child cut a 6-inch circle out of posterboard. Use a hole punch to punch holes around the edge of the circle and punch two holes, about 1 inch apart, in the center of the circle. Let the children decorate their circles with felt-tip markers. Thread a 16-inch piece of string through the center holes of each child's circle and tie the ends together. Show the children how to "wind up" their circles by moving their strings in a circular motion. Then show them how to pull their strings tight to make their circles hum.

Wind and Air Experiments

Give each child a straw, a cotton ball and a scrap of paper. Let the children experiment with the items to answer the following questions: "Can you feel air?" (Blow through your straw against your hand.) "Can you make a cotton ball move without touching it?" (Blow on it through your straw.) "Can you pick up a small piece of paper with a straw?" (Place one end of your straw on the top of the paper and suck on the other end.)

WIND

Wind Facts

Share these facts about wind with the children:

 Air cannot be seen, but it is all around us.

 Wind is air that is moving fast.

 Wind makes such things as windmills, kites and clouds move.

 Wind is an important part of our weather.

 A weather vane shows which way the wind is blowing.

The Wind Roars

Read the sentences below and let the children act them out. Ask the children if they can think of other things that the wind does.

The wind roars like a lion.

The wind hisses like a snake.

The wind gallops like a horse.

The wind is restless like a tiger.

The wind flutters like a butterfly.

I See the Wind

Sung to: "Hush Little Baby"

I see the wind
When the leaves dance by.
I see the wind
When the clothes wave "Hi!"
I see the wind
When the trees bend low.
I see the wind
When the flags all blow.

I see the wind
When the kites fly high.
I see the wind
When the clouds float by.
I see the wind
When it blows my hair.
I see the wind
Most everywhere!

Jean Warren

Streamers in the Wind

Give each child two crepe paper streamers, about 3 feet long, and a dowel or a cardboard paper towel tube. Have the children tape their streamers to their dowels or tubes. Then let them experiment with moving their streamers in the wind as they parade around outside.

Variation: Give the children plastic lids with the centers cut out. Let them attach crepe paper streamers and bells to their lids. Or attach crepe paper streamers to loops of yarn.

Children's Books:
- *Letter to Amy*, Ezra Jack Keats, (Harper, 1968).
- *Who Took the Farmer's Hat?*, Joan Nodset, (Harper, 1963).

Contributors:
Heather Hogg, Sussex, New Brunswick
Colraine Pettipaw Hunley, Doylestown, PA
Ellen Javernick, Loveland, CO
Inez Stewart, West Baraboo, WI
Kristine Wagoner, Federal Way, WA

Zipper Rubbings

Set out a variety of zippers. Let the children place pieces of white paper over the zippers and rub across their papers with crayons. Encourage them to fill their papers with different colored zipper rubbings.

Zipper Bag Game

Place an object in a cloth bag that has a zipper. Give the bag to a child. Have him or her feel the object through the cloth and try to guess what it is. Then have the child unzip the bag and take out the object. Put another object in the bag and let another child have a turn.

Traveling Bag

Set out a small zippered traveling bag and items you might need when you travel, such as a comb, a toothbrush, a pair of socks and a map. Have each child in turn select an item and say, "On my trip I am going to take my _____." Then have the child unzip the bag, place the item in it and zip the bag closed.

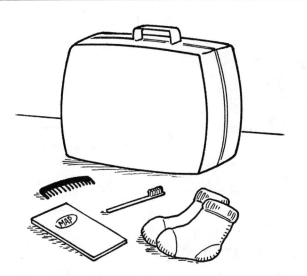

Zipper Table

Set out a variety of objects that have zippers, such as a backpack, a duffel bag, a purse, a sleeping bag and a jacket or other item of clothing. Let the children practice zipping and unzipping the zippers.

Zipper Practice

Dress up a teddy bear in a child's jacket that has a large zipper. Let the children take turns zipping and unzipping the bear's jacket.

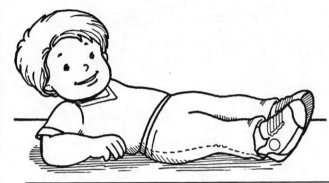

Zipper Legs

Have the children lie down on the floor. Ask them to listen carefully. When you say "Zip up," have them bring their legs together. When you say "Unzip," have them spread their legs apart.

Zip Your Lips!

Sung to: "If You're Happy and You Know It"

If you're loud and you know it, zip your lips!
If you're loud and you know it, zip your lips!
If you're loud and you know it,
Then your mouth will surely show it.
If you're loud and you know it, zip your lips!

Jean Warren

Zipped-Up Snacks

Serve the children such snacks as pretzels, crackers, fruit slices or vegetable sticks in "zip-lock" sandwich bags. Let the children practice "zipping" and "unzipping" the bags while they eat their snacks.

The Zipper Man

Sung to: "The Muffin Man"

Do you know the zipper man,
The zipper man, the zipper man?
Do you know the zipper man?
He loves to zip and zip.

He has a zipper coat,
A zipper coat, a zipper coat.
He has a zipper coat
That he can zip and zip.

He has two zipper boots,
two zipper boots, two zipper boots.
He has two zipper boots
That he can zip and zip.

He has a zipper tent,
A zipper tent, a zipper tent.
He has a zipper tent
That he can zip and zip.

He has a zipper bag,
A zipper bag, a zipper bag.
He has a zipper bag
That he can zip and zip.

He has some zipper pants,
Some zipper pants, some zipper
    pants.
He has some zipper pants
That he can zip and zip.

Jean Warren

Children's Books:
- *Dinosaurs Travel*, Marc Brown,
  (Little, 1988).
- *My Mom Travels a Lot*, Carolyn Bauer,
  (Warne, 1981).

INDEX

Activities, songs and new ideas to use right now are waiting for you in every issue of the Totline Newsletter.

Each issue puts the fun into teaching with 24 pages of challenging and creative activities for young children, including open-ended art activities, learning games, music, language and science activities.

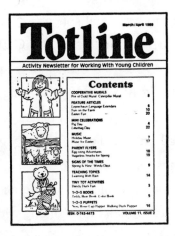

Sample issue $1.00

One year subscription (6 issues) $15.00

Beautiful bulletin boards, games and flannelboards are easy with Totline Patterns.

You won't want to miss a single issue of Totline Patterns with 3 large sheets of patterns delightfully and simply drawn. Each issue includes patterns for making flannelboard characters, bulletin boards, learning games and more!

Sample issue $2.00

One year subscription (6 issues) $18.00

ORDER FROM:
Warren Publishing House, Inc. • P.O. Box 2250, Dept. B • Everett, WA 98203

Totline Books

Super Snacks – 120 seasonal sugarless snack recipes kids love.

Teaching Tips – 300 helpful hints for working with young children.

Teaching Toys – over 100 toy and game ideas for teaching learning concepts.

Piggyback Songs – 110 original songs, sung to the tunes of childhood favorites.

More Piggyback Songs – 195 more original songs.

Piggyback Songs for Infants and Toddlers – 160 original songs, for infants and toddlers.

Piggyback Songs in Praise of God – 185 original religious songs, sung to familiar tunes.

Piggyback Songs in Praise of Jesus – 240 more original religious songs.

Holiday Piggyback Songs – over 240 original holiday songs.

1•2•3 Art – over 200 open-ended art activities.

1•2•3 Games – 70 no-lose games for ages 2 to 8.

1•2•3 Colors – over 500 Color Day activities for young children.

1•2•3 Puppets – over 50 puppets to make for working with young children.

1•2•3 Murals – over 50 murals to make with children's open-ended art.

1•2•3 Books – over 20 beginning books to make for working with young children.

Teeny-Tiny Folktales – 15 folktales from around the world plus flannelboard patterns.

Short-Short Stories – 18 original stories plus seasonal activities.

Mini-Mini Musicals – 10 simple musicals, sung to familiar tunes.

Small World Celebrations – 16 holidays from around the world to celebrate with young children.

Special Day Celebrations – 55 mini celebrations for holidays and special events.

"Cut & Tell" Scissor Stories for Fall – 8 original stories plus patterns.

"Cut & Tell" Scissor Stories for Winter – 8 original stories plus patterns.

"Cut & Tell" Scissor Stories for Spring – 8 original stories plus patterns.

Seasonal Fun – 50 two-sided reproducible parent flyers.

Theme-A-Saurus – the great big book of mini teaching themes.

Theme-A-Saurus II – the great big book of more mini teaching themes.

Alphabet and Number Rhymes – reproducible take-home books.

Color, Shape and Season Rhymes – reproducible take-home books.

Available at school supply stores and parent/teacher stores or write for our FREE catalog.

Warren Publishing House, Inc. • P.O. Box 2250, Dept. B • Everett, WA 98203